BEAUTIFUL BREADS

AND

FABULOUS FILLINGS

THE BEST SANDWICHES *in* AMERICA

MARGAUX SKY

PHOTOGRAPHS BY RON MANVILLE

RUTLEDGE HILL PRESS®
Nashville, Tennessee
A Division of Thomas Nelson Publishers
Since 1798

www.thomasnelson.com

Published by Rutledge Hill Press, a Division of Thomas Nelson, Inc., P.O. Box 141000,
Nashville, Tennessee 37214.

Rutledge Hill Press books may be purchased in bulk for educational, business,
fund-raising, or sales promotional use. For information, please e-mail
SpecialMarkets@ThomasNelson.com.

Library of Congress Cataloging-in-Publication Data

Sky, Margaux, 1954–
    Beautiful breads and fabulous fillings : the best sandwiches in America /
by Margaux Sky.
        p. cm.
    Includes index.
    ISBN 1-4016-0250-9 (hardcover)
    1. Sandwiches. 2. Bread. 3. Cookery, American. I. Title.
    TX818.S625 2006
    641.8′4—dc22   2006004862

Printed in Perú

06 07 08 09 10—5 4 3 2

DEDICATED

to

JOSEPH R. SCHWABA

Thanks for the benefits of your knowledge, Dad.

I'll always love you.

CONTENTS

PREFACE

Many years ago, my father gave me a book called *Beard on Bread* by James Beard. He gave it to me because he considered James Beard an authority on the oldest and most enjoyable food in life: bread. I still have the book though I've long ago made every recipe it contained. As my father respected Mr. Beard as an expert, so I regarded my father. His creativity embraced my heart, and that which he held dear, I shared with him. Consequently, these two men, unknowingly, through a trickle affect, impressed upon me a love of bread and a creative culinary imagination.

My father and I shared a dream of opening a bakery some day and having a cookbook of our own. Before that dream could be realized my father passed away. I ventured the dream alone, but, instead of a bakery, I found myself with a full blown restaurant with a concentration on sandwiches. With any culinary creation of mine, flavor is a must, so I focused on an assortment of wonderful flavors to enhance the bread. I did this by creating unique sauces and fillings. As a result, some beautiful breads and fabulous fillings have been teamed up to make outstanding sandwiches.

How did I come to do a book about sandwiches? In short, my sister, Mary Bennett, asked me to cater a lunch she was having. Mary doesn't like to cook or bake, and she and her husband, Tim, (who cooks turkey burgers and hamburgers and little else) had just moved into their new house. Mary called and asked if I would make some sandwiches, a few salads, and some desserts for her guests, among whom was Oprah Winfrey.

Little did I know that Oprah would be so taken with my Curried Chicken on Spicy

White Pepper-Jack Bread sandwich that she would rave about it on her TV show. She made such a big deal about it that I now call the sandwich the "O" Special.

People worldwide have contacted me wondering if it's possible to ship the sandwich through the mail. In a way, it is. It's now possible to fill those requests by doing this book which will allow others to make the "O" Special sandwich at home. Let me point out, however, if you're like Mary who prefers not to bake or cook, the breads and sauces and many of the other products in this book may be obtained by contacting www.margauxsky.com. They can be shipped directly to you. Check out my website for further details.

This book is the culmination of a dream seed that was planted so long ago, and it couldn't have come to pass without the help of many people. So much credit goes to my father, Joseph R. Schwaba, who taught me much of what I know about baking and cooking. Without his guidance, love, imagination, and the insistence that fun and a good sense of humor be at hand while in the kitchen, I may never have understood that work should be joyful and life sustaining.

Sis Schwaba (Mom), thank you for the regular boosts to my confidence and enough love and support to get me through the trying times—all of them. You cannot truly know how much you mean to me and how much I love you (even if you do use Bisquick)! I am eternally appreciative of and grateful to you.

Mary Bennett, thanks for thinking of me when the opportunity to serve lunch at your home in San Luis Obispo presented itself. Your kindness, belief, and undying support have made my life richer in so many wonderful ways! I love you. I am eternally appreciative of and grateful to you. And Tim Bennett, equally loved, thanks for your wisdom, nurturing, and guidance in business matters and for maneuvering my fits and bursts of confusion into calmer waters that foster reasonable thinking and peaceable action. Thanks for the ever-flowing good advice. I am eternally appreciative of and grateful to you.

Oprah Winfrey, thanks for your great appreciation and love of food, for challenging my ambitions and imagination, and for the golden opportunity to expand one simple sandwich into a commodity of businesses. Thanks for tossing me a wild card in this interesting game of life. I am eternally appreciative and grateful to you.

To my kids, Deja, Otis, Katie, and Melody, thank you for all the peace, love, laughter, and joy you give me.

I am grateful to all the people at DuPree/Miller & Associates and Rutledge Hill Press who've worked on this book. Thank you Michael Broussard and Nena Madonia for being such magnificent agents, helping me through the procedures, honoring my gut instincts and talents, and suggesting I follow and use them. Thanks for your patience with me. I hope for and look forward to future projects together. And Jan Miller, thanks for bringing me on board at DuPree, Miller & Associates, the greatest literary agents on earth. Annabelle at DuPree/Miller & Associates, I love you! Geoff Stone, thanks so much for the masterful editing of this book. I really appreciate your hard work and what I thought was already great, you've made even better! And Pamela Clements, thank you so much for making possible the opportunity to do a book with Rutledge Hill Press. This has been a fantastic and exciting experience.

Margaret Johnson, thanks for the jump-start on this book.

Ron Manville, thanks for photography that drools with an exactness of color and intoxicates with a "come hither" look.

Jeanette Vigne, Brittnie Bennett, Nadine Gunderson, Dan Lewis, and J. P. Bennett thanks for the never-ending cheerleading and constant friendship, regardless of my tantrums.

Lisa, Michael, and Rowan Toke, Jeanne and Barry Labarbera, Jules and Brenda Hoch, thanks for loving my food creations and for your endless support of my love to explore new recipes, use you all as guinea pigs, and pitching my wares to friends, family, and the public. Shevan Sullivan of Anam-Cre Art Studio in San Luis Obispo,

California, thank you for use of your store's awesome and spirited handmade bowls, plates and cups. Thank you, Tsurugi's Japanese Restaurant in San Luis Obispo for use of your scalloped ramekins. Thank you, Porch, Home, and Garden in San Luis Obispo for use of your colorful plates, bowls, and place mats. Thank you, Michael Ackerman-Artist-San Luis Obispo for use of your imaginative, handcrafted tables and fascinating art work. Thank you, Tricia Higgins of Life's Imperfect Designs in Chicago for use of your attractive and innovative table dressings, runners, napkins, and place mats. Thank-you all for your contributions which have assisted enhancing the beauty of the sandwiches and foods in this book.

God, thanks and appreciation for my talents, my life, and the people and animals with whom you endlessly bless me. Thanks for my angelic bodyguards. Thanks for your guidance, friendship, and love.

To all, I couldn't have completed this book without each and every one of you. My appreciation for your love and support is deeply felt. To all of you, free meals as long as I'm alive and cooking! Thanks again everybody!

Please enjoy all of the meals in this book!

INTRODUCTION

Beautiful Breads and Fabulous Fillings: The Best Sandwiches in America boasts gorgeous breads like Horseradish Parmesan, Spicy White Pepper-Jack, Roasted Red Pepper Brie Mint, and Honey Whole Wheat—and they all bear hints of my father's creativity. His passing on to me of his talents and the love of cooking are such blessings in my life. Not a day goes by that I'm not amazed at what I learned as a young child, when my goal was simply to enjoy the friendship and love of my father. That friendship, as well as a shared love of food, has brought me to an unexpected and successful career in middle age.

I began baking and cooking nearly forty-seven years ago. My father was my instructor, and his river of knowledge flowed constantly, with a great emphasis on imagination, flavor, color, and lots of fun.

Quite often, people ask me which culinary school I attended. At first I would tell them I didn't go to culinary school, but now I answer, "The Joseph R. Schwaba Institute of Culinary Creations."

When they ask where it is located, I tell them, "Chicago, Illinois." That's where I spent my childhood and learned my trade. Of course, nobody has ever heard of that school. Inwardly, I smile. No Joseph R. Schwaba Institute of Culinary Creations exists.

Complementing the breads and fillings are fabulous sauces, such as Lavender Mint Love Sauce, Sweet Horseradish Sauce, Creamy Candied Carrot Sauce, Tangy Apricot-Pineapple Sauce, Red Wine and Mustard Vinaigrette Dressing, and others. You'll find my finest bread and sauce creations in this book, and all of them complement meat, fruit, fish, poultry, and vegetables. Some of the sauces are delicious even over desserts like ice cream and pie.

Beautiful Breads and Fabulous Fillings: The Best Sandwiches in America is geared toward both the great love affair America has with sandwiches and my own personal passion for them. The recipes are a testament to the heart and soul that are necessary for excellence, even in the art of sandwich making.

Whether you're attracted to the sandwiches, desserts, salads, or soups, you'll have fun bringing these healthful, beautiful breads, fabulous fillings, and more to the table for yourself, family, and friends. Remember, part of the applause and appreciation for great food comes from those who understand you've taken the time—in a hurried world—to prepare a flavorful meal especially for them.

Sometimes rushing meals onto the table is an unrewarding task, understandably, since fast foods, canned foods, and frozen dinners can lack nutrition, presentation, and beauty. Rushed meals also give testimony to how insatiable a meal can be. Preparing a meal worth remembering is one of life's sweet pleasures. Both the act of preparing the meal and enjoying a well-prepared meal stays with the heart and soul forever. When you take the extra time to create a meal with taste and flair, the memories stay with you forever. A nice presentation of a delicious meal says that you took the time because you love family or guests. It brings happiness to those for whom you've created the meal. That's why taking time to create a centerpiece of a meal sticks with the senses and lingers in the memory of any who see and eat the food creations.

Bread making can be daunting, but it can also be extremely rewarding, and the taste simply can't be beat. Fans will become addicted to your breads. In fact, let me suggest you make four loaves at a time, which is just as easy as making one, because you can freeze the extra loaves. The rest—sauces and fillings—are a breeze to muster up in only minutes. If you don't have the temperament for made-from-scratch cooking, you can purchase many of the breads, sauces, and mixes found in this book at **www.margauxsky.com**.

Bread baking truly is an enjoyable and rewarding process, so luxuriate in it by putting on your favorite music, your most comfortable clothes, a good cup of coffee or tea or a glass of wine, and infuse feelings of happiness and love into your food. It's sure to spread to those you serve.

Healthy eating and thinking to you! May prosperity, peace, creativity, imagination, joy, abundance, and devotion be yours.

TIME SAVERS

Getting It Out

Before you jump in, get out your supplies and ingredients. It's a great time saver to assemble all the ingredients you'll need for the recipe and put them on the counter near your workspace. That way, they're at hand, and you won't repeat the monotonous and frustrating actions of running back and forth.

Putting It Away

My father taught me this, and I'm so glad he did: put away what you've finished using. If you're done with the butter, back in the fridge it goes. If you're done with the curry, put it back on the spice rack. There are good reasons for this: it's out of your way, giving you more room with which to work and you know you've used it, meaning that you are less likely to re-use it. We're all a little forgetful at times, especially beginners. That's why you want to bring everything you need to your workspace and put each item away as soon as you've finished. Believe me, you'll be glad you did.

Clean as You Go

Along the same lines, it's also a good idea to wash dishes as you go. Why should you try not to let them pile up in the sink? If you need a particular measuring cup or spoon at the bottom of the sink, you must remove everything to get the one you want. Then you'll need to wash it, because now it's covered not only with its original chocolate mess, but also butter, salt, pesto sauce, and onions. Wash or rinse it immediately for the next use, and things will go more smoothly.

After you get all your ingredients out, fill the sink (or a large basin) with hot, soapy water. That way you can easily clean your dirty dishes as you go. If you wash or rinse your utensils and bowls as you go, you have what you need at hand on a rack or towel. When you've put the final touches on your creation and into the oven it goes, turn around and your dishes are done! If you usually let them pile up in the sink, as I have maddeningly done, instead try washing them—not to mention wiping the counters—as you go. You'll be surprised at the time and frustration it saves. In a restaurant it's different, because most commercial kitchens have several sets of everything. In a home, that's not usually the case, and digging around in the sink for a measuring spoon can drive you bonkers.

Clean as you go!

WHAT TO USE

In this next section, I'd like to offer my own personal suggestions which have been helpful to me. It is my firm belief that fresh foods are not only more flavorful but more nutritious as well. I also suggest you use fresh herbs over dried as they have more flavor. I am also a strong advocate of using olive oil instead of refined corn oil or using butter as opposed to margarine. Olive oil and butter are more natural fats and easier for your body to use, and they also taste better.

Fresh Over Packaged

Be a stickler for "real" ingredients. Avoid using canned goods, although they can be a convenience and sometimes a necessity. In general, I frown on canned and frozen foods because they tend to be either extremely salty or flavorless. And often they lack the essential nutrients of fresh foods. In addition to better flavor and nutritional value, texture is often considerably more appealing with fresh ingredients.

Herbs and Spices

How do you know which spices to use? Certain spices are naturally more nutritious than others (such as sea salt compared to table salt), but, honestly, most people are unable to detect a difference in flavor between the two. Still, certain spices have greater mineral value and are healthier for you.

Fresh herbs are great in any food, from salads to snacks. You can chop them, grill them in olive oil, salt and pepper them, and put them in a bottle and store them into the fridge. Don't ever discard fresh herbs. Instead be creative. They're good on popcorn, pastas, and even buttered and grilled bread. Depending on which herbs you've prepared, they can be good with a dish of ice cream (e.g., fresh mint).

Common sense tells us that if we pulverize our own spices, our meals will have increased flavor and texture. If you aren't that ambitious, though, then at least buy the freshest spices you can find. Many health food stores carry spices fresher than the typical grocery store, but whatever you use will do fine. Your family and friends will appreciate the meal nonetheless, and most people cannot tell the difference between fresh and not-quite-as-fresh.

Suffice it to say it's always best to use a fresh and natural product, but don't let alternatives stop you from creating a great meal. Remember, the real key to exciting meal preparation is imagination.

Oils

Experts today suggest that we cut down on our intake of trans fatty acids. According to fitnessandfreebies.com "several decades of research show consumption of trans fatty acids promotes heart disease, cancer, diabetes, immune dysfunction, and obesity and reproductive problems." In the past people frowned on butter because of its fat content. However, butter does not contain the bad trans fats that are found in margarine and vegetable oils. It not only gives fabulous flavor to foods, but it turns out, in moderation, it is better for you. The American Heart Association recommends that "naturally occurring unhydrogenated oil be used when possible and attempts made to substitute unhydrogenated oil for hydrogenated or saturated fat." I'm in good company when I recommend using olive oil and butter—substances your body can use—over margarine and vegetable oil, which are filled with harmful trans fatty acids.

Utensils

It's surprising how personal the utensils you use in the kitchen can become. If you cook for any amount of time, you'll find yourself with a favorite mixing spoon, serrated knife, or spatula, and nothing else will do. Believe it or not, I even have a favorite spoon to eat my cereal with. People choose favorites all the time, even when it applies to utensils like some of those I'll be discussing such as mixers, bowls, knives, and even the vegetable peeler.

The proper utensils make a good kitchen. Following are the utensils that I prefer, but you should use what you love best. In commercial kitchens anything wooden is against the rules due to potential bacteria and salmonella buildup. That's the lovely thing about your kitchen. In baking and cooking at home, there are no rules. You can use whatever products, utensils, and ingredients you desire just as long as you use your imagination. Personally, I love and prefer wooden utensils. Just make sure you clean them thoroughly with very hot, soapy water after use, and after cutting up raw poultry, it is a good idea to clean your utensils with a little bleach water.

Stand Mixers

You'll probably find you have all the utensils you need for the recipes in this book. Depending on how many loaves you make at one time, you may want to consider a stand mixer suitable for a home; even if you're making as many as four at a time, however, a stand mixer is a convenience, not a necessity.

Look at it this way: kneading dough is a great workout for the arms. If you won't be making more than four loaves, a very large mixing bowl will suffice, and the dough can be manipulated and kneaded by hand on the countertop. The total kneading time will be about four to six minutes when done by hand, but it depends on how much pressure and speed you use.

One of the things I've always loved about making breads *is* the kneading. Rolling the dough over repeatedly in your hands is a sensuous feeling and, as corny as it sounds, you get a real sense of the bread. Machines, like stand mixers, are a must when making massive quantities as we did at the café, but when baking breads at home, I still knead by hand. It's therapeutic for me.

Mixing Bowls and Spoons

You will need a good set of mixing bowls and spoons when baking and cooking. For all practical purposes there is no difference among wooden, glass, steel, or ceramic bowls. You just need the right size bowl to accommodate all the ingredients you'll be putting in it with room to spare to avoid spills.

Standing mixers usually come with a set bowl.

When choosing a bowl with which to work, consider its sturdiness. If you're going to be doing a lot of physical sitrring, you want a sturdy bowl. Some plastic bowls are so flimsy that when you even breathe on them, they go soaring off of the countertop. Plastic bowls are good for microwaving, but over time they can begin to peel. Since you're investing in bowls, I would probably avoid plastic and go for aluminum bowls which are sturdy and durable, however, not microwaveable. For microwaving I recommend glass bowls; they are sturdier than plastic, but be careful as they will break. Since not all ceramic bowls are microwaveable and since they are usually very beautiful I recommend using them for serving. Bottom line, your pocketbook, color scheme, and reasons for use will determine what you end up with.

With mixing spoons, it's pretty much the same game. Strength and durability are what

you want, and you *definitely* want heat-resistant spoons and spatulas. Many manufacturers offer several different size spoons per package, which may cost more, but then you have every size you need. Personally, I prefer wooden spoons over plastic, but when I go with plastic they are always heat resistant.

Measuring Cups and Spoons

Ideally, having many sets of measuring cups and spoons around is great, but remember what I said about the ease and convenience of washing dishes as you go? Some people like several sets of measuring utensils and will do all the dishes at the end. That's fine, too. Whatever suits you.

Measuring cups are measuring cups. I've heard many stories and complaints: glass is better than plastic or plastic is better than glass, a four-cup is better than a two-cup, or a cook should use specific measuring cups for wet and dry ingredients. A measuring cup is a measuring cup. Whatever you use will serve. Don't get caught up in trivialities. Have fun.

Measuring spoons, for the most part, are measuring spoons. However, I do recommend buying measuring spoons that have the numbers etched into the spoon. Ink can fade, making the spoons unusable for measuring. If you get plastic measuring spoons, which work just as well, make sure the measurements are etched into the plastic.

Spatulas/Scrapers

There isn't a way to bake or cook without the aid of spatulas and if there is anything to invest in that's worth spending money on, it's heat resistant plastic spatula scrapers. Plastic scrapers are necessary because they pick up every little spot of food left in a bowl, and there are some out there that can withstand very high temperatures, which allows you to scrape hot ingredients or to even use them while sautéing. When buying plastic, always get the higher grade, high heat-resistant kind. It will last longer and won't contaminate your food by falling apart. Be warned, although heat-resistant spatulas can be pretty pricey, inevitably, you'll leave a spatula resting on a hot pan and will be glad that it can withstand the heat.

Spatula turners are firm and used for flipping burgers, like steel flat-nosed spatulas. They make plastic spatula turners, but I prefer the metal ones. The thing that bothers me about plastic products is that they tend to break easier.

Whisks

You'll want to own some whisks. Smaller whisks can be used in smaller bowls. One large, one medium, and one small whisk should suffice. The large size can be used for mixing flours and grains before adding the wet ingredients. You can mix the dry and wet ingredients with your hands if you really want to get the feel of the dough. Either way, once the wet ingredients are mixed into the flour, you will need to use your hands to knead the dough.

Knives

You'll need sharp knives of different sizes. If you aren't familiar with handling knives, ask your grocery store butcher to show you how to carve meats and ask the staff of the deli section how to chop veggies. Carve or chop anything *away* from your hands and body, not towards them. It's a good idea, even for experts, not to rush when working with knives. Work slowly.

(After all, why not develop a baking and cooking atmosphere that's pleasant and free from hurrying? Rushing, especially with a knife in your hand, increases the likelihood of accidents. Relax, and enjoy.)

Vegetable Peeler

Vegetable peelers are really a breed to themselves. There are only so many to choose from, but the differences are so subtle. It's like needing to get somewhere quickly and deciding whether to skate board or roller skate.

Avoid steel peelers (and whisks) unless they're stainless steel, otherwise, after a few washings, you'll have rust to contend with, and they'll just end up in the garbage. Some people prefer swivel peelers—those with swiveling blades. There are a number of instruments to choose from and most people have a favorite. Find yours, and it'll become a kitchen friend.

Food Processors

Food processors are great for some things, like making nut butters, jams, and various other things, but I don't care for them for prepping vegetables. They always seem to dry out my carrots, onions, and other veggies. At the café we grate our vegetables by hand to keep them juicy and flavorful.

You'll be hard-pressed to find someone who doesn't thrill at receiving a fabulous loaf of homemade bread. It is truly a gift that expresses your caring. Recognize that creating sumptuous breads and meals for you, your family, and your friends is creating gifts of love. Preparing great foods takes time, but the breads in this book are worth it.

Follow the directions carefully and methodically. Don't skip any step, such as letting the dough rise. Be sure to preheat the oven completely before baking the bread, and don't be afraid of the yeast factor. Once the aroma of fresh bread fills your home, you'll experience delight and a sense of accomplishment.

You'll find that every time you serve one of the sandwiches in this book, your family and friends will be amazed at the intense flavors. More often than not, you'll share the gift by breaking bread. During the assembly and consumption of breads, sauces, and fillings, your loved ones will express appreciation—and appreciation is another one of those things that makes life richer. When you recognize how happy you've made the recipient, you'll want to continue giving without recompense.

Love should be expressed, and food can be the greatest show on earth.

A LITTLE ABOUT BREAD

Bread has been an essential part of the human diet for centuries. Early societies formed a bowl in heavy boulders and used small rocks to grind wheat and seeds in the hollow of the boulder. They then combined these grains with water to form versions of breads.

Native Americans used a similar process in milling their wheat, corns, and millet into thicker flat breads similar to modern day pita breads. They stuffed the flat breads with buffalo meat and vegetables native to the surroundings, then added spices and flavorings such as turmeric, maple syrup, cayenne, and salt.

Today, we use mortars and pestles to grind our spices, or we buy them at the grocery store. We use electric mixers to fashion our dough, or we go to the nearest bakery for bread. Today, we are blessed with so many varieties of flours and spices from which to choose. It's interesting to look back and see how far we've come from the days of boulder baking.

When Bread Became King

Yeast is a single-celled microbe, and one gram contains 20 billion single-celled microorganisms. Hieroglyphs show that five thousand years ago, Egyptians discovered yeast—actually *barm,* a fluid yeast resulting from making beer and wine. Beer barm causes bread to rise into lighter, fluffier loaves. (Wine barm was not as desirable for bread making because of its bitterness.)

In the seventeenth century, the Paris Faculty of Medicine, evidently influenced by a biblical passage of St. Paul's in which alcohol was perceived to be a corrupt substance, outlawed beer barm and wine barm yeasts. It was believed they might contribute to the decline of human health and interfere with an individual's religious focus. Bakers ignored the law and continued to create breads using beer barm—without significant opposition. As far as the Faculty of Medicine goes, my guess is that even its members wanted fabulous bread, so they turned a blind eye to some of society's questionable assumptions and let the bakers create.

As the beer barm (yeast) reacts with water and flour, the dough expands like a tremendous hot air balloon. Heat, which builds up during this chemical reaction explodes, like a volcano erupting lava, and releases carbon dioxide throughout the dough. The result: the dough expands enormously. Slice a piece of bread and you'll see tiny air pockets where the carbon dioxide expanded to create a higher, fluffier bread. If you prepare a dough and don't use it within a few days, you'll notice a powerful aroma of yeast. Taste it and you'll recognize a more intense development of yeast. I find this an overwhelming intrusion to the taste buds, but my father loved breads empowered with yeast.

Appreciation for the lighter bread took off, and cultures worldwide began consuming this bakery marvel. With the introduction of yeast, which changed the function and appearance of bread, a love affair with this divine aliment was born. Bread (even white, which is far underrated in the U.S.) has been and always will be one of humans' main food desires. It is clearly the most versatile food ever imagined and the most ancient comestible creation.

CHAPTER ONE

Beautiful and Unique White Breads

For centuries, people around the world have been eating white bread. White flour contains calcium, folic acid, iron, potassium, protein, thiamine (B1), riboflavin (B2), and niacin (B3). White flour can be either bleached or unbleached. A flour that is bleached is whiter than unbleached flour and contains chemical agents, which are added not only to whiten the flour but to preserve and prolong its shelf life.

Many of the breads in this book are "filled breads," which can be tricky to get out of the pan because of the tendency of the filling to stick to the pan. Simply take a knife and go along the edges of the pan to free the loaf. If the bottom sticks, gently nudge it free with the knife. Once you replace the loaf after checking its doneness, it will conform to the pan again as it cools.

Basic White Bread

Four loaves at a time is easy, and nine more recipes in the book require this dough. You'll have fun making all of them, and you can always freeze the loaves and give them as gifts later.

2	tablespoons yeast	16	cups all-purpose flour plus extra for dusting
4	cups warm milk		
4	cups warm half-and-half	3 1/2	tablespoons salt
1/2	cup (1 stick) butter, melted	2	eggs
1/2	cup powdered sugar	4	tablespoons water

> In a large bowl, dissolve the yeast in the milk and half-and-half. Let stand for 5 minutes, until the yeast is foamy. Add the butter and mix with a whisk. Add the powdered sugar and mix well to break up any clumps.

> In a large bowl (or stand mixer), combine the flour and salt. Slowly add the liquid mixture to the flour mixture and knead well. If you're using a stand mixer, knead for 3 to 4 minutes. If you're kneading by hand, knead for 4 to 7 minutes. Keep the dough moist for a soft, tender bread.

> Place the kneaded dough in a generously buttered bowl, cover with a towel, and let rise in a warm, dry place for 60 minutes.

> Punch the dough down with your fist, and divide it into 4 portions.

> Generously butter four 9-inch loaf pans, form the portions of dough into loaves, and place them in the pans. Let them rise another 45 minutes. After the dough has risen a second time, you can portion it into four freezer bags and store it in the freezer for future use.

> Preheat the oven to 400 degrees.

> Beat together the eggs and water to make an egg wash. Brush the egg wash over the dough and bake for approximately 1 hour.

> Carefully remove a loaf from a pan and tap the bottom of the loaf. If it sounds hollow, they're done. If not, continue to bake, checking the loaves every few minutes. When done, remove all pans from the oven, and cool them for 30 minutes. Remove the loaves from the pans and transfer them to a wire rack. Cool for another 30 minutes before slicing.

Yield: 4 loaves

Horseradish-Parmesan Bread

Even many people who don't like horseradish love this popular bread. Its flavor is subtle and dizzying.

	Basic White Bread Dough (see page 3)	1/4	teaspoon salt
2	tablespoons olive oil	2	cups shredded Parmesan cheese
1 1/2	cups Sweet Horseradish Sauce (see page 82)	1	egg
1	tablespoon Lawry's lemon pepper	2	tablespoons water

> Roll out a softball-size piece of dough from the White Bread recipe (one-quarter of the batch) into a 9 x 11-inch rectangle so that the long side is perpendicular to your body.

> Spread the olive oil over the dough. Spread the Sweet Horseradish Sauce evenly over the dough. Sprinkle the lemon pepper and salt over the horseradish sauce and then the Parmesan cheese over the spices.

> Generously butter a 9-inch loaf pan.

> With your hands, tightly roll the dough into a loaf, with the rolling action going away from your body. To hold in the fillings, fold the outer edges of the dough as you roll.

> Place the dough into the prepared loaf pan seam side down. Place the pan in a warm, dry place and allow it to rise for 60 minutes.

> Preheat the oven to 400 degrees.

> Beat together the egg and water to make an egg wash. Brush the egg wash over the dough. Make three diagonal slits—deep enough to see the filling—across the top of the loaf.

> Bake for approximately 1 hour.

> Remove the loaf from the pan and tap the bottom of the loaf. If it sounds hollow, it's done. If not, continue to bake, checking every few minutes. When the loaf is done, return it to the pan, remove from the oven, and cool for 30 minutes. Remove the loaf from the pan and transfer it to a wire rack. Cool for another 30 minutes before slicing.

Yield: 1 loaf

According to hungrymonster.com, during the building of the Egyptian pyramids centuries ago, the workers were fed radishes, which were known to produce a heightened energy level. They also increased the sex drive, which reasonably could have caused frustration, consequently stimulating the desire and ability to work harder and faster. Perhaps Cleopatra's reputation as a red hot lover had more to do with her radish intake than anything.

Lavender-Mint Love Bread

The four fresh herbs (in the sauce) in this loaf make for an earthy flavor. It's a rich, powerful bread that goes well with meat, fish, and veggie sandwiches.

	Basic White Bread Dough (see page 3)		
2	tablespoons olive oil	2	cups manchego cheese
1 ½	cups Lavender-Mint Love Sauce (see page 58)	1	egg
		2	tablespoons water

> Roll out a softball-size peice of dough from the White Bread recipe (one-quarter of the batch) into a 9 x 11-inch rectangle so that the long side is perpendicular to your body.

> Spread the olive oil over the dough. Spread the Lavender Mint Love Sauce evenly over the dough. Sprinkle the manchego cheese on top.

> Generously butter a 9-inch loaf pan.

> Tightly roll the dough into a loaf, with the rolling action going away from your body. To hold in the filling, fold in the outer edges of the dough as you roll.

> Place the loaf into the prepared loaf pan seam side down. Place the pan in a warm, dry place and allow the dough to rise for 60 minutes.

> Preheat the oven to 400 degrees.

> Beat together the egg and water to make an egg wash. Brush the egg wash all over the dough. With a sharp knife, cut three lavender-leaf-shaped slits into the dough.

> Bake for approximately 1 hour.

> Ovens vary so test for doneness. Remove the loaf from the pan and tap the bottom of the loaf. If it sounds hollow, it's done. If not, continue to bake, checking every few minutes. When the loaf is done, return it to the pan and cool for 30 minutes. Remove the loaf from the pan and transfer it to a wire rack. Cool for another 30 minutes before slicing.

Yield: 1 loaf

I'm surprised that so few people use lavender in their baking and cooking. It has a fantastic and unique tang that flatters almost any dish. I have lavender plants at home and regularly clip off a branch for cooking. I just finely chop the greens and beautiful purple flowers and sauté them in a little olive oil and salt. Lavender is good with pasta, veggies, meats, salad, grilled bread, salmon, or just about any food. When combined with other herbs, its flavor is absolutely delightful in a subtle, serendipitous way.

Lemon Alive Bread

This bread is tart and delicious and goes wonderfully with fish sandwiches or a single slice of fish grilled as a side to a salad.

Basic White Bread Dough
(see page 3)
2   tablespoons olive oil
1 1/2 cups Lemon Alive Sauce
(see page 60)

1/2   cup lemon zest
2   cups shredded Monterey Jack cheese
1   egg
2   tablespoons water

> Roll out a softball sized piece of dough from the White Bread recipe (one-quarter of the batch) into a 9 x 11-inch rectangle so that the long side is perpendicular to your body.

> Spread the olive oil over the dough, then spread with the Lemon Alive Sauce, followed by the lemon zest and cheese.

> Generously butter a 9-inch loaf pan.

> Tightly roll the dough into a loaf with the rolling action going away from your body. To hold in the filling, fold in the outer edges of the dough as you roll.

> Place the loaf into the prepared loaf pan seam side down. Place the pan in a warm, dry place and allow the dough to rise for 60 minutes.

> Preheat the oven to 400 degrees.

> Beat together the egg and water to make an egg wash. Brush the egg wash all over the dough. Bake the loaf for approximately 1 hour.

> Ovens vary so test for doneness. Remove the loaf from the pan and tap the bottom of the loaf. If it sounds hollow, it's done. If not, continue to bake, checking every few minutes. When the loaf is done, return it to the pan and cool for 30 minutes. Remove the loaf from the pan and transfer it to a wire rack. Cool for another 30 minutes before slicing.

Yield: 1 loaf

The lemon is one of the most popular fruits around but not just for its enticing flavor. Lemon juice is flavorful when made into lemonade, but it's also great for warding off cold sores and sore throats, according to lemonflower.com. Lemon juice and honey in tea or hot water can help to soothe the scratching and aching of a sore throat. Lemons are high in vitamin C and have natural antiseptic qualities. Lemon juice in a glass of water is not only good for digestion, but is also a very good cleansing agent for the body.

Peanut Butter-Chocolate Fudge Bread

This creation is as much a dessert as a bread, although it would work well for a PB&J, too. It's wonderful with the filling in the Garden of Eden on Concord Grape Bread (see page 105) recipe or with just plain honey or jam. Be careful grilling this bread because of the oozing chocolate and peanut butter. You must have your stove on high and sear the bread more than grill it, being careful not to burn the chocolate. Whenever you even get a slight scent of this bread baking, you'll stop what you're doing to head toward the oven.

	Basic White Bread Dough (see page 3)
2	cups peanut butter (or the nut butter of your choice, see page 83)
2	cups Creamy Chocolate Fudge Topping (see page 235)

1	egg
2	tablespoons water
1/4	cup chocolate chips

> Roll out a softball-size piece of dough from the White Bread recipe (one-quarter of the batch) into a 9 x 11-inch rectangle so that the long side is perpendicular to your body.

> Spread the Peanut Butter evenly over the dough. Spread the Chocolate Fudge Topping over the Peanut Butter.

> Generously butter a 9-inch loaf pan.

> Tightly roll the dough into a loaf, with the rolling action going away from your body. To hold in the filling, fold in the outer edges of the dough as you roll.

> Place the loaf into the prepared loaf pan. Place the pan in a warm, dry place and allow the dough to rise for 60 minutes.

> Preheat the oven to 400 degrees.

> Beat together the egg and water to make an egg wash. Brush the egg wash all over the dough. Bake for approximately 1 hour.

> Ovens vary so test for doneness. Remove the loaf from the pan and tap the bottom. If it sounds hollow, it's done. If not, continue to bake, checking every few minutes.

> When the loaf is done, melt the chocolate chips in the microwave and drizzle over the bread. Let the bread cool in the pan for 30 minutes. Then transfer it to a wire rack and cool for another 30 minutes.

Yield: 1 loaf

Homemade bread made with homemade peanut butter (see page 83) and homemade chocolate fudge topping (see page 235). Nothing else to say.

Roasted Red Pepper-Brie-Mint Bread

This bread is outstanding! *The combination of flavors is very unique and surprising. It is one of the most popular breads I make, and the explosion of unexpected flavors makes it a bread hard to forget and easy to crave. It is powerfully tasteful in the most wonderful way served with lamb as a lamb sandwich.*

	Basic White Bread Dough (see page 3)
2	tablespoons olive oil
1 3/4	cups plus 2 tablespoons Real Mint Sauce (see page 75)
1	tablespoon Lawry's lemon pepper

1/4	teaspoon salt
2	Roasted Red Peppers (see page 205), julienned
2	cups chopped or torn Brie cheese

> Roll out a softball-size piece of dough from the White Bread recipe (one-quarter of the batch) into a 9 x 11-inch rectangle so that the long side is perpendicular to your body.

> Spread the olive oil over the dough. Spread the 1 3/4 cups Real Mint Sauce evenly over the dough. Sprinkle the lemon pepper and salt evenly over the Real Mint Sauce. Lay the Roasted Red Peppers side by side on top of the Real Mint Sauce until you've covered most of the dough. Arrange the Brie cheese over the peppers.

> Generously butter a 9-inch loaf pan.

> Tightly roll the dough into a loaf, with the rolling action going away from your body. To hold in most of the fillings, fold the outer edges of the dough as you roll.

> Place the dough into the prepared loaf pan creased side down. Pour the remaining 2 tablespoons Real Mint Sauce on top. Place the pan in a warm, dry place and allow the dough to rise for 60 minutes.

> Preheat the oven to 400 degrees.

> Bake for approximately 1 hour.

> Ovens vary so test for doneness. Remove the loaf from the pan and tap the bottom. If it sounds hollow, it's done. If not, continue to bake, checking every few minutes. When the loaf is done, return it to the pan and cool for 30 minutes. Remove the loaf from the pan and transfer it to a wire rack. Cool for another 30 minutes before slicing.

Yield: 1 loaf

Peppers are known to have many wonderful influences on the body. An important one is their aid in healing respiratory problems and their high volumes of vitamin C. And mint is well known for its calming properties and cool flavor.

Rosemary-Sage White Bread

Clearly, as the title indicates, this bread is dominated by the herbs rosemary and sage. It's an earthy bread with a rich, luxurious flavor which comes through in the sauce and pulls the whole thing together.

	Basic White Bread Dough (see page 3)	1/8	teaspoon salt
1 1/2	cups Rosemary-Sage Sauce (see page 78)	2	cups crumbled goat cheese
1	tablespoon Lawry's lemon pepper	1	egg
1	tablespoon lemon zest	2	tablespoons water

> Roll out a softball-size piece of dough from the White Bread recipe (one-quarter of the batch) into a 9 x 11-inch rectangle so that the long side is perpendicular to your body.

> Spread 1 1/2 cups of the Rosemary-Sage Sauce evenly over the dough.

> Over the sauce, sprinkle the lemon pepper, lemon zest, and salt. Sprinkle the goat cheese over the spices.

> Generously butter a 9-inch loaf pan.

> Tightly roll the dough into a loaf, with the rolling action going away from your body. To hold in most of the filling, fold the outer edges of the dough as you roll.

> Place the dough into the prepared loaf pan seam side down. Place the pan in a warm, dry place and allow the dough to rise for 60 minutes.

> Preheat the oven to 400 degrees.

> Beat together the egg and water to make an egg wash. Brush the egg wash over the dough.

> Bake for approximately 1 hour.

> Ovens vary so test for doneness. Remove the loaf from the pan and tap the bottom. If it sounds hollow, it's done. If not, continue to bake, checking every few minutes. When the loaf is done, return it to the pan and cool for 30 minutes. Remove the loaf from the pan and transfer it to a wire rack. Cool for another 30 minutes before slicing.

Yield: 1 loaf

Native Americans burn sage for its healing, quieting properties, not to mention its soothing aroma. I like to imagine the herb blessing me with its peace.

Salsa Bread

This bread is fabulous for just about any of the sandwiches but especially the Avocado and Melted Swiss Sandwich (see page 87). A close friend of mine likes turkey bacon, apple butter, Swiss cheese, and greens on this bread—with a side of salsa. Opposites attract; apparently, even in food.

	Basic White Bread Dough (see page 3)
2	cups Salsa (see page 59)
2	cups shredded pepperjack cheese
1	egg
2	tablespoons water

> Roll out a softball-size piece of dough from the White Bread recipe (one-quarter of the batch) into a 9 x 11-inch rectangle so that the long side is perpendicular to your body.

> Drain any excess juices from the salsa. Set aside a few tablespoons of both the salsa and the cheese.

> Spread the salsa evenly over the dough. Sprinkle the pepperjack cheese over the salsa.

> Generously butter a 9-inch loaf pan.

> Tightly roll the dough into a loaf, with the rolling action going away from your body. To hold in the filling, fold the outer edges of the dough as you roll.

> Place the loaf into the prepared loaf pan. Place the pan in a warm, dry place and allow the dough to rise for 60 minutes.

> Preheat the oven to 400 degrees.

> Beat together the egg and water to make an egg wash. Brush the egg wash over the dough.

> Bake for approximately 1 hour. During the last 10 minutes of baking time, sprinkle some salsa and cheese over the top of the loaf for distinction.

> Ovens vary so test for doneness. Remove the loaf from the pan and tap the bottom. If it sounds hollow, it's done. If not, continue to bake, checking every few minutes. When the loaf is done, return it to the pan and cool for 30 minutes. Remove the loaf from the pan and transfer it to a wire rack. Cool for another 30 minutes before slicing.

Yield: 1 loaf

Sweet Dough

Sweet dough is the firt dough I created and is extremely versatile. It's the base for my cinnamon rolls, cinnamon-raisin bread, sweet bread, sandwich loaves, and pastries. This dough can be refrigerated for a couple days, but allow it to warm to room temperature before baking.

1	tablespoon yeast
2	cups warm water
1	cup warm milk
1	cup heavy cream
1	cup (2 sticks) butter, melted

1/2	cup sugar
4	eggs, beaten
1	teaspoon vanilla extract
12	cups all-purpose flour (approximately)
1/8	teaspoon salt

> In a large bowl, dissolve the yeast in the water and milk. Add the cream. Let stand for 5 minutes, or until the yeast is foamy.

> Generously grease a large bowl.

> Add the butter, sugar, eggs, and vanilla to the yeast mixture.

> Slowly add the flour and salt to the wet ingredients and mix well.

> Place the dough on a floured countertop or board and knead for 4 minutes.

> Place the dough in the prepared bowl. Place the bowl in a warm, dry place and let the dough rise for 60 minutes. Punch down the dough with your fist and separate into two portions. You can use the dough immediately or refrigerate it for later use.

Yield: 2 melon-size batches
        (8 or 9 pastries per batch)

Pastries are a popular dessert worldwide and, there are probably as many different pastries as there are cafes in the world. I exaggerate only mildly, I'm sure. There are cookies, cakes, pies, puff pastries, French pastries, European pastries, sweet rolls, coffee cakes, and on and on. This sweet dough can be used for many different breads and pastries, as you will see.

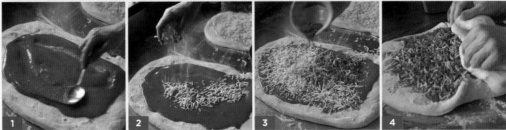

Spicy White Pepper-Jack Bread

Spicy White Pepper-Jack Bread is famous with the "O" Special (aka Curried Chicken on Spicy White Pepper-Jack Bread on page 100). Very popular, but be warned: Spicy White Pepper-Jack Bread is fiery hot! To reduce the spiciness, cut the amount of cayenne to one tablespoon or less, or omit it altogether.

	Basic White Bread Dough (see page 3)
2	tablespoons olive oil
1 1/2	cups Curry Sauce (see page 51)
1 1/2	tablespoons cayenne
1	tablespoon Lawry's lemon pepper
1/4	teaspoon salt
2	cups shredded Monterey Jack cheese
1	egg
2	tablespoons water

> Roll out a softball-size piece of dough from the White Bread recipe (one-quarter of the batch) into a 9 x 11-inch rectangle so that the long side is perpendicular to your body.

> Spread the olive oil over the dough. Spread the Curry Sauce evenly over the dough. Sprinkle the cayenne, lemon pepper, and salt over the Curry Sauce. Sprinkle the cheese over the spices.

> Generously butter a 9-inch loaf pan.

> Tightly roll the dough into a loaf, with the rolling action going away from your body. To hold in the filling, fold the outer edges of the dough.

> Place the loaf into the prepared loaf pan. Place the pan in a warm, dry place and allow the dough to rise for 60 minutes.

> Preheat the oven to 400 degrees.

> Beat together the egg and water to make an egg wash. Brush the egg wash over the dough.

> Bake for approximately 1 hour. During the last 10 minutes of baking time, sprinkle some of the filling over the top of the loaf for distinction.

> Ovens vary so test for doneness. Remove the loaf from the pan and tap the bottom. If it sounds hollow, it's done. If not, continue to bake, checking every few minutes. When the loaf is done, return it to the pan and cool for 30 minutes. Remove the loaf from the pan and transfer it to a wire rack. Cool for another 30 minutes before slicing.

Yield: 1 loaf

Three Cheese Bread

I love rainy days, grilled bread, hot tea, a good book, my favorite sofa, and a soft throw. This bread is tops in any sandwich category, but fits my needs simply grilled with butter.

	Basic White Bread Dough (see page 3)		
	Basic White Bread Dough (see page 3)	2	tablespoons Lawry's lemon pepper
1	cup crumbled goat cheese	1/2	teaspoon salt
1	cup shredded sharp Cheddar cheese	1	egg
1	cup shredded manchego cheese	2	tablespoons water

> Roll out a softball-size piece of dough from the White Bread recipe (one-quarter of the batch) into a 9 x 11-inch rectangle so that the long side is perpendicular to your body.

> Spread the goat cheese, Cheddar cheese, and manchego cheese over the dough. Sprinkle the lemon pepper and salt evenly over the cheeses.

> Generously butter a 9-inch loaf pan.

> Tightly roll the dough into a loaf, with the rolling action going away from your body. To hold in the filling, fold the outer edges of the dough as you roll.

> Place the dough into the prepared loaf pan seam side down. Place the pan in a warm, dry place and allow the dough to rise for 60 minutes.

> Preheat the oven to 400 degrees.

> Beat together the egg and water to make an egg wash. Brush the egg wash over the dough. Make three diagonal slits—deep enough to see the filling—across the top of the loaf.

> Bake for approximately 1 hour.

> Ovens vary so test for doneness. Remove the loaf from the pan and tap the bottom. If it sounds hollow, it's done. If not, continue to bake, checking every few minutes. When the loaf is done, return it to the pan and cool for 30 minutes. Remove the loaf from the pan and transfer it to a wire rack. Cool for another 30 minutes before slicing.

Yield: 1 loaf

Many people consume cheese for its flavor alone; it's delicious on sandwiches and fries. (One of my favorite light meals is steamed broccoli with melted sharp Cheddar cheese.) Cheese is well known for its significant amounts of calcium and protein, but it also offers the nutrients zinc, vitamins A and B12, phosphorous, and riboflavin (vitamin B2). It may also stimulate the flow of saliva, which is said to increase buffering capacities that can neutralize plaque acids, which destroy teeth and gums.

Concord Grape Bread

This bread is unusual, and I enjoy the perplexed look on people's faces when they see the name. It's fabulous for many sand-wiches, especially the Garden of Eden (see page 105) for which I specifically created it. It makes a superb French toast, too. Because this bread is very soft, you may think it's under baked. Be certain to check for the hollow sound. When using it for French toast, soak it as long as possible in the batter.

1	tablespoon yeast		1	cup powdered sugar
2	cups warm vanilla soy milk		1/2	cup (1 stick) butter, melted
1	(8-ounce) container boysenberry yogurt		9	cups all-purpose flour (approximately)
1	(32-ounce) jar Concord grape jelly		1	tablespoon salt

> Generously grease a large mixing bowl and two loaf pans and set aside.

> In a large bowl, dissolve the yeast in the soy milk. Let it stand for 5 minutes, or until the yeast is foamy.

> Add the yogurt, jelly, powdered sugar, and butter and mix well.

> In another large bowl, combine the flour and salt.

> Slowly add the wet ingredients to the dry ingredients and mix well with your hands. This dough is extremely wet.

> Transfer the dough to the prepared bowl. Place the bowl in a warm, dry place and allow the dough to rise for 60 minutes.

> Separate into two portions and transfer each portion into the prepared loaf pans. Place the pans in a warm, dry place and allow the dough to rise for 60 minutes.

> Preheat the oven to 375 degrees and bake the bread for about 1 hour.

> Ovens vary so test for doneness. Remove a loaf from the pan and tap the bottom. If it sounds hollow, it's done. If not, continue to bake, checking every few minutes. When the loaf is done, return it to the pan, remove the other pan from the oven, and cool for 30 minutes. Remove the loaves from the pans and transfer them to a wire rack. Cool for another 30 minutes before slicing.

Yield: 2 loaves

The Concord Grape was developed by Ephraim Wales Bull in 1849 after he tried over 20,000 seedlings to come up with the perfect Concord Grape in Concord, Massachusetts, according to wikipedia.org. By 1869, the Concord Grape found its way into the hands of Dr. Thomas Welch, who figured out that through pasteurization, he could eliminate the fermentation that turned the grapes into wine, and thereby successfully turn the grapes into a juice.

English Muffins

Watch that the heat isn't too high. If it is, the muffins will bake too quickly on the outside but remain doughy inside. If the muffins are browning too quickly, decrease the heat, and turn them over regularly. They should be firm, but retain the softness associated with breads. After only a day or two they can get rather hard. Even then, however, they're fabulous once they are toasted or grilled. To get that "holey" texture for which English muffins are famous, split them with a fork rather than slicing with a knife. See pages 144–149 for my wonderful Stuffed English Muffin Sandwiches.

1	tablespoon yeast
1/2	cup warm water
2	cups warm milk (or half-and-half for richer tasting muffins)
1/2	cup (1 stick) butter, melted
2	eggs, beaten
1/2	cup powdered sugar
8	cups all-purpose flour (approximately)
1 1/2	teaspoons salt

> In a large mixing bowl, dissolve the yeast in the water and milk. Let stand for 5 minutes, until the yeast is foamy.

> Add the butter, eggs, and powdered sugar to the yeast mixture, and mix well.

> In another large bowl, combine the flour and salt.

> Slowly add the wet ingredients to the dry ingredients, and mix well with your hands. Place the dough on a floured countertop or board and knead for 4 to 6 minutes.

> Spread the dough with your hands until about 1/2 inch thick.

> Using a 3-inch round cutter of some sort (e.g. the top to a large mustard jar) cut the dough into muffin-sized rounds. Make as many rounds as you can. Allow them to rise for 60 minutes.

> On a greased griddle or skillet over medium-low heat, cook the muffins about 7 minutes per side, or until just golden.

> Slice the muffins and toast in the toaster or grill on the griddle.

Yield: 8 muffins

The English are famous for the "crumpet," which is a milk, flour, salt, and yeast combination that is baked on a griddle in special metal crumpet rings, according to englishmuffins.com. They mildly resemble English Muffins, but English Muffins also have eggs, butter, and sugar in them. Crumpets are smooth on the bottom, but the top is peppered with tiny holes. English muffins are also baked on a griddle, but are smooth on both sides and should be pried open with a fork in order to produce an uneven middle, which, when toasted or grilled, gives it a crunchy texture.

Sweet French Loaf

Because this bread is very soft, you may think it's under baked. Check for the hollow sound. This bread becomes bulky, which is part of its great appeal. It has a slightly sweet flavor, so if you're a butter nut like I am, spread some over a warm piece of this bread and devour. It is not an authentic French bread. The reason I call it such is because it makes the most fabulous French toast you'll eat. Ever! (See page 219 for French toast.) For those who are sensitive to dairy products or on a vegan diet, this is vegan bread.

1	tablespoon yeast
2	cups warm water
1 1/2	cups warm vanilla soy milk
1	cup powdered sugar

1/2	cup packed brown sugar
8	cups all-purpose flour (approximately)
1	tablespoon salt

> In a medium bowl dissolve the yeast in the water and soy milk. Let stand for 5 minutes, or until the yeast is foamy.

> Add the powdered sugar and brown sugar to the yeast mixture.

> In a large bowl combine the flour and salt. Slowly add the wet ingredients to the dry ingredients and, using your hands, mix well.

> Place the dough on a floured countertop or board and knead for 4 minutes. Keep the dough moist for soft, tender bread.

> Generously butter a baking sheet. Free form the dough onto the baking sheet. Slice a long, deep gash in the center of the dough. Let it rise for about 60 minutes.

> Preheat the oven to 400 degrees. Bake on the baking sheet for 45 minutes. Reduce the heat to 350 degrees and bake another 15 minutes.

> Ovens vary so test for doneness. Tap the bottom of the loaf. If it sounds hollow, it's done. If not, continue to bake, checking every few minutes. When the loaf is done, cool for 30 minutes before slicing.

Yield: 1 large loaf

Maple Merlot Bread

This is a unique tasting bread. Although the alcohol is baked out, it still has a wine flavor. This is a bread I typically snack on when I'm hungry for just a little something, because I love its flavor—both on its own and with a sandwich. I prefer the bread grilled with butter, and I drizzle a little maple syrup or honey over it.

1	tablespoon yeast
2	cups warm half-and-half
2	cups warm red merlot wine
3/4	cup plus 2 tablespoons maple syrup
1/2	cup (1 stick) butter, melted

9	cups all-purpose flour (approximately)
3/4	cup packed brown sugar
1 1/2	tablespoons salt
1	cup shredded Monterey Jack cheese

> In a large bowl, dissolve the yeast in the half-and-half. Let stand 5 minutes, until the yeast is foamy. Add the merlot, 3/4 cup of the maple syrup, and butter.

> In another large bowl combine the flour, brown sugar, and salt and mix with a wire whisk.

> Slowly add the wet ingredients to the dry ingredients and mix well.

> Place the dough on a floured countertop or board, and knead for 4 minutes. Keep the dough moist for a soft, tender bread. Put the dough in a well buttered bowl and let rise for 60 minutes.

> Punch down the dough with your fist and separate it into two portions.

> Generously butter two 9-inch loaf pans.

> Form the two dough portions into loaves and place them in the prepared loaf pans.

> Make a deep cut, almost to the pan, in each loaf. Into each, pack 1 tablespoon of the maple syrup and 1/2 cup of the cheese. Close and smooth the top of the bread.

Merlot wine is made from a red grape brought to France in the first century, according to wineintro.com. The merlot grape doesn't age well so was coupled with other varieties like a cabernet and other French Bordeaux wines. It's only recently that merlot has gone solo, proving itself to be an outstanding and delicious wine in its own right. Mellower and less biting, it's great with red meats and has a reputation as being one of the best red wines to complement indulgent chocolate.

> Place the pans in a warm, dry place, and let the dough rise for 45 to 60 minutes.

> Preheat the oven to 400 degrees. Bake the loaves for about 1 hour.

> Ovens vary so test for doneness. Remove a loaf from the pan and tap the bottom. (If the syrup has caused the bread to stick, slide a sharp knife along the edges of the pan, gently nudging the loaf.) If it sounds hollow, it's done. If not, continue to bake, checking every few minutes. When the loaf is done, return it to the pan, remove the other pan from the oven, and cool for 30 minutes. Remove the loaves from the pans and transfer them to a wire rack. Cool for another 30 minutes before slicing.

Yield: 2 loaves

Cinnamon-Raisin Bread

Everybody has a favorite cinnamon bread or toast. Try this recipe; my guess is it'll take over your number one position! It's soft, gooey, and delicious.

1	cup (2 sticks) butter
2	cups packed brown sugar
1	cup white sugar
1 1/2	to 2 tablespoons cinnamon

1	batch Sweet Dough (see page 17)
1	to 2 cups raisins

> In a medium bowl melt the butter. Set aside 2 tablespoons for later. Add the brown sugar and white sugar and mix well. Add the cinnamon and mix thoroughly.

> Roll out the Sweet Dough into a 9 x 11-inch rectangle so that the long side is perpendicular to your body.

> Spread the cinnamon mixture evenly over the dough. Add the raisins. Drizzle the remaining 2 tablespoons of butter over the raisins.

> Generously butter a 9-inch loaf pan.

> Tightly roll the dough into a loaf, with the rolling action going away from your body. To hold in the filling, fold in the outer edges of the dough as you roll.

> Place the dough in the prepared loaf pan seam side down. Place the pan in a warm, dry place and let the dough rise for 60 minutes.

> Preheat the oven to 375 degrees. Bake the bread for 50 to 60 minutes.

> Ovens vary so test for doneness. Remove the loaf from the pan and tap the bottom of the loaf. If it sounds hollow, it's done. If not, continue to bake, checking every few minutes. When the loaf is done, return it to the pan, remove from the oven, and cool for 30 minutes. Remove the loaf from the pan and transfer it to a wire rack. Cool for another 30 minutes before slicing.

Yield: 1 loaf

Cinnamon comes in two forms: ground or stick. It also comes in two varieties: Ceylon and Chinese. Ceylon is a slightly sweeter variety, but is also the more difficult one to find in stores. According to whfoods.com, the aroma of cinnamon is now known to heighten brain activity and utilize to greater degrees the ability for cognizant processing and increased memory. Consuming cinnamon is also said to "improve the body's ability to utilize blood sugar". Mixed in with tea, its said to release an actual warming effect on the body, causing it relief from undesired stress and tension.

CHAPTER TWO

Beautiful and Unique Brown Breads

Brown breads include wheat, rye, buckwheat, grains, oats, and others. They're denser and more fibrous than white breads and have greater amounts of protein, and the flavor is more intense and earthier. By far, they are healthier breads to consume.

Brown breads are gaining in popularity because they are an extremely nutritious and tasty breads. Yet not all brown breads hold the place in people's hearts that whole wheat bread does. For instance, I adore rye bread, but I know scores of people who do not!

Basic Whole Wheat Bread

This whole wheat bread is wonderful! Make all four loaves and share them with your family, friends, and neighbors. They'll thank you for the thought and love you for the gift. Read on for some interesting interpretations of this whole wheat recipe.

2	tablespoons yeast
5	cups warm water
2	cups warm milk
2	cups warm half-and-half
3/4	cups packed brown sugar
1	cup (2 sticks) butter, melted
3/4	cup honey

1 1/2	teaspoons vanilla extract
18	cups whole wheat flour (approximately)
3 1/2	tablespoons salt
1	egg
2	tablespoons water

> Generously grease a large bowl and set aside.

> In a very large bowl, dissolve the yeast in the water, milk, and half-and-half. Let stand for 5 minutes, or until the yeast is foamy. Add the brown sugar, butter, honey, and vanilla to the yeast mixture and mix well.

> In another very large bowl (or stand mixer), combine the whole wheat flour, and salt.

> Slowly add the wet mixture to the dry mixture and mix well. If you're using a stand mixer, knead for 3 to 4 minutes. If you're kneading by hand, turn the dough onto a floured countertop or board, and knead for 4 to 7 minutes. Keep the dough moist for a soft, tender bread.

> Place the kneaded dough in the prepared bowl. Place the bowl in a warm, dry place and let the dough rise for 60 minutes.

> Punch down the dough with your fist and divide it into 4 portions.

> Generously butter four 9-inch loaf pans, form the dough into loaves and place them in the pans. Let them rise another 60 minutes.

> Preheat the oven to 375 degrees.

Some wheat flours are minus the bran and germ making them, theoretically, a "white" flour. A whole grain whole wheat bread is whole wheat flour which consists of the entire wheat kernel: the bran, the germ, and the endosperm.

> Beat together the egg and water to make an egg wash. Brush the egg wash over the dough and bake the loaves for approximately 1 hour.

> Carefully remove a loaf from the pan and tap the bottom. If it sounds hollow, it's done. If not, continue to bake, checking the loaves every few minutes. When a loaf is done, return it to the pan, remove all pans from the oven, and let them cool for 30 minutes. Remove the loaves from the pans and transfer them to a wire rack. Cool for another 30 minutes before slicing.

Yield: 4 loaves

Cranberry, Currants, and Cream Cheese Bread

You can use fresh cranberries and currants without having to worry about extra moistness. If you're going to use dried cranberries and currants, soak them in warm water first to make them softer and less chewy. Some people (like me) like the chewy version. This bread is interesting with any of the veggie sandwiches and quite tasty with the meat sandwiches, too.

2	tablespoons butter
1 1/2	cups dried cranberries
1 1/2	cups dried currants
16	ounces cream cheese

1/4	cup plus 3 tablespoons maple syrup
	Basic Whole Wheat Bread (see page 34)
1	egg
2	tablespoons water

> Melt the butter in a skillet over medium heat. Add the cranberries, currants, cream cheese, and 1/4 cup of the maple syrup. Mix well and cover. Let simmer for 5 to 10 minutes, stirring frequently.

> Generously butter a 9-inch loaf pan.

> Roll out a softball-size piece of dough from the Whole Wheat Bread recipe (one-quarter of the batch) into a 9 x 11-inch rectangle so that the long side is perpendicular to your body.

> Spread the remaining maple syrup over the dough. Then spread the mixture in the skillet evenly over the dough.

> Tightly roll the dough into a loaf rolling away from your body. To hold in the filling, fold in the outer edges of the dough as you roll.

> Place the dough into the prepared loaf pan seam side down. Place the pan in a warm, dry place and allow the dough to rise for 60 minutes.

> Preheat the oven to 375 degrees. Beat together the egg and water to make an egg wash. Brush the egg wash over the dough. Make three diagonal slits—deep enough to see the filling—across the top of the loaf.

> Bake for approximately 1 hour.

> Remove the loaf from the pan and tap the bottom of the loaf. If it sounds hollow, it's done. If not, continue to bake, checking every few minutes. When the loaf is done, return it to the pan, remove from the oven, and cool for 30 minutes. Remove the loaf from the pan and transfer it to a wire rack. Cool for another 30 minutes before slicing.

Yield: 1 loaf

Currents are high in vitamin C, the highest of all temperate fruits, according to tonytanillo.com. Not only do currants taste delicious, they're fabulous for your health.

Ginger-Goat Cheese Whole Wheat Bread

Basic Whole Wheat Bread Dough
(see page 34)

1 1/2 cups Ginger Sauce (see page 61)

1 cup Candied Ginger Pieces
(see page 61)

2 cups crumbled goat cheese (or to taste)

1 tablespoon Lawry's lemon pepper

1/2 teaspoon salt

1 egg

2 tablespoons water

> Roll out a softball-sized piece of dough from the Whole Wheat Bread recipe (one-quarter of the batch) into a 9 x 11-inch rectangle so that the long side is perpendicular to your body. Form a crust around the edges in order to hold the Ginger Sauce.

> Spread the Ginger Sauce over the dough. Sprinkle the lemon pepper and salt over the sauce.

> Spread the Candied Ginger Pieces on top. Sprinkle the goat cheese over the Ginger Pieces.

> Generously butter a 9-inch loaf pan.

> Tightly roll the dough into a loaf, with the rolling action going away from your body. To hold in the fillings, fold the outer edges of the dough as you roll.

> Place the dough into the prepared loaf pan seam side down. Place the pan in a warm, dry place and allow the dough to rise for 60 minutes.

> Preheat the oven to 375 degrees.

> Beat together the egg and water to make an egg wash. Brush the egg wash over the dough. Make three diagonal slits—deep enough to see the filling—in the top of the loaf.

> Bake the loaf for 55 to 60 minutes.

> Remove the loaf from the pan and tap the bottom. If it sounds hollow, it's done. If not, continue to bake, checking every few minutes. When the loaf is done, return it to the pan, remove from the oven, and cool for 30 minutes. Remove the loaf from the pan and transfer it to a wire rack. Cool for another 30 minutes before slicing.

Yield: 1 loaf

There are a hundred ways to use ginger, and in this book, I've given you a couple. According to wikipedia.org, ginger stimulates the saliva glands causing the mouth to produce copious saliva for more mouthwatering treats. It's also noted for soothing illness caused by motion sickness. Morning sickness also is calmed by the gingerroot.

Honey-Nut Whole Wheat Bread

Honey and nuts have been a long-time coupling and, when combined with this fabulous wheat bread, the result is practically a meal in itself. Many people use this bread with vegetable fillings for their sandwiches. The combined flavors of meat and nuts are very compelling though. In other words, this bread is great with any sandwich filling.

	Basic Whole Wheat Bread Dough	1	cup finely chopped mixed nuts
2	tablespoons butter	1	egg
3/4	cups honey	2	tablespoons water
1	teaspoon flour		

> Roll out a softball-size piece of dough from the Whole Wheat Bread recipe (one-quarter of the batch) into a 9 x 11-inch rectangle so that the long side is perpendicular to your body.

> Melt the butter in a skillet over medium heat. Add the honey, flour, and nuts. Mix well and cook, stirring constantly, until the honey thickens.

> Spread the mixture evenly over the dough.

> Generously butter a 9-inch loaf pan.

> Tightly roll the dough into a loaf, with the rolling action going away from your body. To hold in most of the fillings, fold in the outer edges of the dough as you roll.

> Place the dough into the prepared loaf pan seam side down. Place the pan in a warm, dry place and allow the dough to rise for 60 minutes.

> Preheat the oven to 375 degrees.

> Beat together the egg and water to make an egg wash. Brush the egg wash over the dough. Make three deep slits—deep enough to see the filling—in the top of the loaf.

> Bake the loaf for 55 to 60 minutes.

> Remove the loaf from the pan and tap the bottom of the loaf. If it sounds hollow, it's done. If not, continue to bake, checking every few minutes. When the loaf is done, return it to the pan, remove from the oven, and cool for 30 minutes. Remove the loaf from the pan and transfer it to a wire rack. Cool for another 30 minutes before slicing.

Yield: 1 loaf

Honey and nuts go together like any natural coupling that comes to your mind: salt and pepper, turkey and dressing, milk and cookies, cake and ice cream. Honey contains antioxidants to equal those of spinach, apples, oranges, or strawberries. Almonds are one of the healthiest nuts a person can eat. I've been hearing that all of my life, especially from my father. Almonds have been known to reduce levels of "bad" cholesterol and contain healthy unsaturated fats.

Rosemary-Sage Whole Wheat Bread

This has an even earthier flavor than the Rosemary-Sage White Bread, because of the rich grain flavor inherent in whole wheat. It's luxurious and pleasing in texture and taste.

	Basic Whole Wheat Bread Dough	1/8	teaspoon salt
1 1/2	cups Rosemary-Sage Sauce (see page 78)	2	cups goat cheese
1	tablespoon Lawry's lemon pepper	1	egg
1	tablespoon lemon zest	2	tablespoons water

> Roll out a softball-size piece of dough from the Whole Wheat Bread recipe (one-quarter of the batch) into a 9 x 11-inch rectangle so that the long side is perpendicular to your body.

> Spread the Rosemary-Sage Sauce evenly over the dough.

> Sprinkle the lemon pepper, lemon zest, and salt over the dough, followed by the goat cheese.

> Generously butter a 9-inch loaf pan.

> Tightly roll the dough into a loaf, with the rolling action going away from your body. To hold in most of the fillings, fold in the outer edges of the dough as you roll.

> Place the dough into the prepared loaf pan creased side down. Place the pan in a warm, dry place and allow the dough to rise for 60 minutes.

> Preheat the oven to 375 degrees.

> Beat together the egg and water to make an egg wash. Brush the egg wash over the dough. Make three diagonal slits—deep enough to see the filling—across the top of the loaf.

> Bake for 55 to 60 minutes.

> Remove the loaf from the pan and tap the bottom of the loaf. If it sounds hollow, it's done. If not, continue to bake, checking every few minutes. When the loaf is done, return it to the pan, remove from the oven, and cool for 30 minutes. Remove the loaf from the pan and transfer it to a wire rack. Cool for another 30 minutes before slicing.

Yield: 1 loaf

Goat cheese and rosemary make a fantastic culinary cruise for the taste buds, but there are some other interesting things about them, too. Students in ancient Greece wore loose wreaths of rosemary around their necks because of its ability to uplift the memory. It is also strongly associated with the goddess of love, Venus, and as a result, is often used at weddings as a representation of fidelity. Goat's cheeses have been around for over 12,000 years and are considered one of the healthiest cheeses for the body. Lots of protein, magnesium, and calcium and since goat cheese is lactose free, it's much easier for the human body to digest.

Rye Bread

Homemade rye bread is one of my favorites. If you like rye bread and you've never had homemade, do yourself a favor and make this. This rye bread is fabulous as an herb bread, too! All you need to do is add 1 tablespoon of dill weed and 1 cup of chopped fresh basil (or 2 tablespoons of dried sweet basil) to the flour mixture. I love it with the herbs. It gives the bread an even earthier flavor. This bread enhances so many sandwiches, but especially the Reuben (see page 132). Great for sandwiches, it's also fabulous just buttered and grilled and then buttered again!

8	tablespoons yeast		2	tablespoons caraway seed
6	cups warm water		2	tablespoons salt
2	tablespoons olive oil		20	cups rye flour (approximately)
2	cups packed brown sugar		1	egg
1	tablespoon fennel seed		2	tablespoons water

> In a large bowl, dissolve the yeast in the water. Let it stand for 5 minutes, or until the yeast is foamy. Add the olive oil and brown sugar.

> In another large bowl combine the fennel seed, caraway seed, salt, and rye flour. Slowly pour the liquid mixture into the flour mixture and mix well. Keep the dough moist for a soft, tender bread.

> Pour the dough onto a rye-floured countertop or board and knead for 4 to 7 minutes. Separate it into 2 portions.

> Generously grease two baking sheets.

> With your hands, form the dough into loaves on the baking sheet. (If you prefer a smooth surface, wet your hands and smooth the surface of the bread to your liking.)

> Place the baking sheet in a warm, dry place and let the dough rise for 60 minutes.

> Preheat the oven to 375 degrees.

> Beat together the egg and water to make an egg wash. Brush the egg wash over the dough. Make three deep slits into the top of each loaf.

> Bake for 45 to 55 minutes.

> Remove a loaf from the pan and tap the bottom of the loaf. If it sounds hollow, it's done. If not, continue to bake, checking the loaves every few minutes.

> Cool for 50 minutes.

Yield: 4 loaves

Rye flour, like other flours, is graded based on its milling process. Naturally, rye flour with the bran intact has greater dietary fiber and more protein. The coarsest rye meal is pumpernickel, which contains the entire whole grain and can be found in dark rye, medium rye, or white rye. Rye berries (kernels) are used in the same fashion as the wheat berries. Rye is a flour which hasn't the amount of gluten that a wheat flour has and is, therefore, often coupled up with wheat flour or an all-purpose flour when baking bread.

Brown Harvest Bread

This bread happens to be a favorite of a woman I consider a very dear angel. For her, in addition to the recipe above, I add a cup of macadamia nuts and 2 cups of raisins per loaf. She loves raisins, and the extra creaminess of the macadamia nuts give the bread an even more distinctive flavor. It's like a dessert. She loves it with peanut butter and honey!

1	tablespoon yeast		1/2	cup roasted pine nuts
5	cups warm water		1/2	cup roasted almonds
3/4	cup molasses		1/2	cup roasted cashews
1/2	cup packed brown sugar		1/2	cup Candied Walnuts (see page 203)
1/2	tablespoon olive oil		1/2	tablespoon salt
9	to 10 cups whole wheat flour		1	egg
1	(16-ounce) package 10-grain mix		2	tablespoons water
2	cups quick-cooking oats			

> In a large bowl, dissolve the yeast in the water. Let it stand for 5 minutes, or until the yeast is foamy. Add the molasses, brown sugar, and olive oil.

> In another large bowl, combine the whole wheat flour, 10-grain mix, oats, pine nuts, almonds, cashews, walnuts, and salt.

> Slowly add the wet mixture to the dry mixture and mix well. Turn the dough onto a lightly wheat-floured countertop or board.

Knead the dough for 4 to 7 minutes. Keep the dough moist for a soft, tender bread.

> Separate the dough into two portions.

> Generously grease 1 to 2 baking sheets, depending on their sizes. With your hands form the sections of dough into round loaves on the baking sheet. Place the sheets in a warm, dry place and let the dough rise for 60 minutes.

> Preheat the oven to 375 degrees.

Molasses was a prized commodity in Colonial trade, so much so that the "founders of the colony of Georgia promised each man, woman, and child who endured a year in Georgia 64 quarts of molasses as a reward," according to grandmamolasses.com. I would have stayed.

Molasses is also a very popular sweetener, oftentimes used in place of or alongside sugar. It is pure and natural sugarcane juices that have been reduced to achieve the results of perfect color, consistency, and unique flavor. Some brands of molasses are pure, unrefined cane juice, meaning none of the sugar has been extracted. It is very high in iron, calcium, and potassium. It's even higher in manganese and copper.

> Beat together the egg and water to make an egg wash. Brush the egg wash over the dough. Make three deep slits—deep enough to see the filling—in the top of each loaf.

> Bake the loaves for 45 to 55 minutes.

> Tap the bottom of one of the loaves. If it sounds hollow, it's done. If not, continue to bake, checking every few minutes.

> Let the loaves cool for 45 minutes before slicing.

Yield: 2 loaves

CHAPTER THREE

Sauces, Dressings, and Butters

Although I created certain sauces to go with particular sandwiches, mixing and matching will be inevitable—and exciting. Foods you wouldn't necessarily think of coupling often make for creative, mouthwatering remembrances and mealtime fun.

The sauces go with the sandwich recipes. There is generally one-quarter cup of sauce for each sandwich. Be sure to store the extra sauce in an airtight container in the refrigerator. Most of the sauces will keep for about one week in the refrigerator. But they are so good, they probably won't last that long.

Curry Sauce

Thousands of restaurants throughout the world boast their own curry sauce renditions, and many are divine. I wanted to make my own version, and it turned out unusual and flavorful. This is the sauce in the famous "O Special" (aka Curried Chicken on Spicy White Pepper-Jack Bread on page 100).

3	cups honey
1 1/2	cups deli or spicy mustard
2	tablespoons Lawry's lemon pepper
2	tablespoons curry powder
1/4	teaspoon salt

> In a large bowl combine the honey, mustard, lemon pepper, curry powder, and salt. Mix well. Serve with the Curried Chicken sandwich. Also try it with any meat, veggie, rice, or noodle dish.

> Extra sauce should be stored in an airtight container in the refrigerator. When you're ready to use it, heat it in the microwave or a skillet over medium-low heat.

Yield: About 4 cups

Curry is actually a blend of many different spices—typically including turmeric, chiles, coriander, ginger, garlic, and cumin just to name a few. Many claim, including devout Ayurvedics (people devoted to the Indian, holistic form of medicine called Ayurveda), that its bank of spices offers many healing agents. For instance, Ayurvedics claim that it aids blood purification and new blood tissue growth, relieves congestion, lowers cholesterol levels, and even acts as a natural antibacterial. This I know: curry powder gives food both a fabulous flavor and clears my sinuses.

Coffee Liqueur Mushroom Sauce

One day at the grocery store in the liquor aisle, a bottle of coffee liqueur caught my eye. I glanced in my cart at the bag of mushrooms. Coffee liqueur and mushrooms! (That's what I love about those little "angel nudges" that prompt me to stop and consider combinations I might not otherwise.) I experimented with the ingredients and came up with this Coffee Liqueur Mushroom Sauce. Its flavor is extremely intense, and it's simply stupendous with meat, so for those with shy taste buds, get ready for an awakening.

2	tablespoons butter
3	cups sliced mushrooms
1/2	cup chopped shallots or leeks
1/2	cup chopped red onions
1	cup coffee liqueur

2	to 3 tablespoons half-and-half
1	to 2 tablespoon packed brown sugar
	Lawry's lemon pepper (to taste)
	Salt (to taste)
1	tablespoon all-purpose flour

> In a large skillet, melt the butter over medium heat. Add the mushrooms, shallots, and onions. Cook until the onions are caramelized (a translucent tan) and the mushrooms are dark brown, about 7 minutes.

> Add the liqueur, half-and-half, brown sugar, lemon pepper, and salt. Mix very well. Add the flour and mix well with a wire whisk until the flour is no longer lumpy.

> Increase the heat to medium high and bring the mixture to a boil. When it thickens to desired consistency, remove it from the heat. Serve immediately with the Beef Tenderloin sandwich on page 92.

> Extra sauce should be stored in an airtight container in the refrigerator. When you're ready to use it, heat it in the microwave or a skillet over medium-low heat. Add more coffee liqueur or half-and-half to thin the sauce, if needed.

Yield: About 3 cups

Coffee Liqueur came from the Caribbean. Its distinct flavor has given boost to many a delicious meal. It's typically pretty expensive. When cooked with foods, the alcohol is cooked off, but the flavor remains in full force.

Creamy Candied Carrot Sauce

The Creamy Candied Carrot Sauce idea came to me during an extended stay in Las Vegas a few years ago. I'd found a cute little café that I frequented for lunch. I tried different items, but preferred an appealing vegetarian sandwich. The bread was nothing spectacular—clearly store-bought. The veggies were fresh, but what caught my attention was the sumptuous sauce. When I returned home to California, I began experimenting with something I thought would be great on a full veggie sandwich: I adore carrots, the base for this sauce.

2	cups shredded carrots
1	cup sweetened condensed milk
1/4	cup powdered sugar
1	tablespoon fresh lemon juice
1	tablespoon honey
1/2	teaspoon Lawry's lemon pepper
1/8	teaspoon salt

> In a large bowl mix together the carrots, milk, sugar, lemon juice, honey, lemon pepper, and salt. Serve with the Garden Patch sandwich on page 106.

> Extra sauce should be stored in an airtight container in the refrigerator.

Yield: About 3 cups

Carrots are, of course, a great source of vitamin A and beta-carotene, but they're also great fiber for the digestive system. Their only drawback is that some are bland and flavorless. Always buy carrots with the greens if possible, and ask the produce manager for the newest shipment. While fresh carrots with greens aren't always sweet, the chances of getting sweet carrots from a fresh batch are greater

Creamy Viognier and Pineapple Sauce

I love viognier wine. Hidden within lurks a slight flavor of pineapple. I got the idea for this sauce at a friend's dinner party when I was inspired by a glass of viognier and her marvelous chicken marsala. I imagined a creamy viognier sauce with a strong hint of pineapple spilled over chicken tenders on open-faced French bread. (I prefer tenders, rather than breasts.) And the Creamy Viognier and Pineapple Sauce was born. It's to live for! It's not only great over chicken tenders; it's also good with fish, meat, and veggie dishes.

1/4	cup (1/2 stick) butter
1	cup sliced mushrooms
1/2	cup chopped red onions
2	cups viognier
2	to 3 teaspoons chicken bouillon granules
1	cup half-and-half
1	cup pineapple juice
1	tablespoon packed brown sugar
1	tablespoon Lawry's lemon pepper
1	teaspoon salt
1	cup diced fresh pineapple

> In a deep skillet, melt the butter over low heat. Add the mushrooms and onions, increasing the heat to medium, and let them cook until the mushrooms are a deep, golden brown and the onions are caramelized (a translucent tan), about 7 minutes. Stir frequently to avoid burning.

> Add the wine, chicken bouillon, half-and-half, pineapple juice, brown sugar, lemon pepper, and salt to the skillet and cook, stirring constantly, until the mixture begins to boil. Let it boil for 1 minute and then reduce the heat to low. Let the mixture simmer until slightly thickened—not too thick—about 10 minutes. Add the pineapple and mix well.

> Serve immediately as part of the Chicken in a Creamy Viognier and Pineapple Sauce Sandwich on page 150.

> Extra sauce should be stored in an airtight container in the refrigerator. When you're ready to use it, heat it in the microwave or a skillet over medium-low heat.

Yield: About 4 cups

Viognier wine is a wonderful aromatic blend of peaches, apricots, and violets, with a buttery pineapple bouquet. It tastes marvelous! It's one of my favorite wines, reminding me of crisp autumn days and nights. According to tablascreek.com, its origins may date back to the Roman Empire, but nobody seems to know for sure. There was a time the viognier grape was grown only in the Rhone Valley; however, as time passed, its popularity has grown. Now, the grape is grown in California as well, apparently only since the 1980s! It's a relatively new wine to the United States but is becoming an increasingly cosmopolitan drink.

Guacamole

Everyone I know has made guacamole—and every time it's been delightful. Mine is, too!

6	avocados, peeled and chopped
3	tablespoons fresh lemon juice
3	tablespoons fresh orange juice
1/4	cup finely diced red onions
1/4	cup finely diced tomatoes

2	tablespoons lemon zest
1	teaspoon Lawry's lemon pepper
1/2	teaspoon salt
1/8	teaspoon cayenne pepper

> In a large bowl combine the avocados, the lemon juice, and the orange juice. Mash together with a fork for chunky guacamole. For creamy guacamole use an electric mixer. If you need to, add a little more lemon juice.

> Add the onions, tomatoes, lemon zest, lemon pepper, salt, and cayenne pepper and mix well with a wooden spoon or spatula.

> Serve with the Avocado and Melted Swiss sandwich on page 87. It's also good with chips and salsa.

> Store any extra guacamole in an airtight container in the refrigerator. Cover with plastic wrap, pressing it drectly into the surface of the guacamole to prevent it from turning brown.

Yield: About 2 1/2 cups

Avocados are known as the "alligator pears" because of their crinkly skin and the shape, which resembles an alligator's head. Avocados are pretty much available year round but are at their peak during the summer months. They are a good source of vitamin K, potassium, and vitamin E. They lend a smooth and creamy flavor and texture to any meal from soups to salads to dips. In my opinion, they are one of the tastiest fruits going.

Lavender Mint Love Sauce

Lavender has an unusual and addicting flavor. This sauce goes well with any meat, fish, or veggie dish. It's also delicious with vanilla ice cream, soup, and fruit! The aroma of lavender oil is heavenly, and the oil is popular as an aid in body massages. When my sister Tricia gives me a massage, I request lavender oil. My sister Mary says that placing lavender oil on your temples and any pulse points of the body creates a sensation of peace and relaxation. The lavender plant, as well as producing an oil that can be worn as a perfume, is also a great herb for cooking. This sauce will calm you all the way to your stomach.

1	(20-ounce) container plain yogurt (about 2 ½ cups)	2	tablespoons chopped fresh mint
¾	cup soft cream cheese	1	tablespoon chopped fresh basil
¾	cup Sobe Green Tea	½	tablespoon chopped fresh sage
2	tablespoons honey	2	teaspoons curry powder
3	tablespoons chopped fresh lavender	⅛	teaspoon salt

> In a large bowl combine the yogurt, cream cheese, green tea, and honey. Mix well.

> In a small bowl combine the lavender, mint, basil, sage, curry, and salt.

> Add the herb mixture to the yogurt mixture and mix well.

> Serve at room temperature with the Flaked Salmon sandwich on page 99.

> Store in an airtight container in the refrigerator.

Yield: About 6 cups

Lavender is blooming in popularity and it's about time. It's useful in so many ways, from cooking to potpourris. It dates back to the Roman Empire, where it was used as an herb with and in which they washed, hence the meaning of lavender: "to wash". Lavender is also now cited as being a stress and headache reliever, which I can testify to. Just dab a little lavender oil on your pulse points and inhale its wonderful aroma. One other great thing about lavender: it makes great lavender lemonade. Just add lavender stems to your hot water until it cools and proceed with making your favorite lemonade.

Salsa

I don't know two people who make salsa alike. It's another one of those fun and easy sauces with which to experiment. Salsa is easy to make on the spur of the moment and is a great dip for any chip. For the Avocado and Melted Swiss Sandwich on Salsa Bread, see page 16.

3	cups diced tomatoes	1/2	cup freshly squeezed lemon juice
1	cup diced cilantro	1/2	cup shredded manchego cheese
1	cup diced red onions	1	teaspoon Lawry's lemon pepper
1/2	cup diced green bell pepper	1	teaspoon salt
1/8	cup lemon zest	1/8	teaspoon cayenne pepper

> Let the tomatoes stand in a bowl for 10 minutes. In a separate bowl, mix together the cilantro, onions, bell pepper, lemon zest, lemon juice, cheese, lemon pepper, salt, and cayenne pepper.

> Drain the tomatoes. Add them to the other ingredients and mix well. Serve with the Avocado and Melted Swiss sandwich on page 87 or as an appetizer with chips.

> Store any extra salsa in an airtight container in the refrigerator.

Yield: About 3 cups

Minty Yogurt Sauce

This sauce is marvelous on any sandwich, but I like it best with Chicken Salad in Minty Yogurt Sauce (see page 96).

2	cups vanilla yogurt	1	teaspoon vanilla extract
1	cup finely diced fresh mint leaves	1/8	teaspoon salt
1	teaspoon Lawry's lemon pepper		

> In a large bowl, mix together the yogurt, mint, lemon pepper, vanilla, and salt. Serve with any lamb dish or with the Chicken Salad.

> Store any extra sauce in an airtight container in the refrigerator.

Yield: About 2 cups

It may be in my head but I prefer to heat all my extract in the microwave for about 6 seconds to take away the bite. I do this for recipes that aren't cooked.

Lemon Alive Sauce

Lemons are beautiful, especially in my cobalt blue bowl on the kitchen island. Gorgeous, plump, bright yellow lemons. I keep another bowl of fruit to eat: apples, peaches, plums, and oranges, but the blue bowl is the lemon bowl. If I put a fruit other than lemons in it, I'd be breaking up a heavenly match. This sauce is scrumptious on breads as a spread, on chips as a dip, and even splashed into soup. It's delicious over fish and other seafood dishes, such as the Flaked Salmon Sandwich on page 98 and the Herb Grain Breaded Fish Sandwich on page 113.

1	tablespoon olive oil
2	tablespoons (about 2 cloves) chopped fresh garlic
1	cup lemon yogurt
2	tablespoons butter, melted
1/2	cup fresh lemon juice (juice from about 3 lemons)
1/8	cup freshly grated lemon zest
1	tablespoon Lawry's lemon pepper
1	teaspoon salt
1/2	teaspoon dried basil

> Heat the olive oil in a small skillet over medium heat. Add the garlic and sauté until lightly browned.

> In a saucepan or skillet over medium heat, combine the yogurt, butter, lemon juice, lemon zest, lemon pepper, salt, basil, and garlic. Bring to a boil while stirring with a whisk. Reduce the heat to low.

> Simmer until the mixture thickens, about 10 minutes, stirring frequently.

> Remove from the heat and serve warm.

> Store any extra sauce in an airtight container in the refrigerator. Warm leftover sauce in the microwave, and mix well before using.

Yield: About 1 1/2 cups

Lemons are an effective facial cleanser. Grate lemon peel into a small bowl, squirt in a little lemon juice and an equal amount of water, and mix well. Wash your face with soap and water, and dry it well. Press the lemon peel mixture to your face and scrub softly for a minute or so. Rinse with cool water. It's cleansing and refreshing and leaves a splendid citrus aroma on the skin.

Ginger Sauce and Candied Ginger Pieces

I'm crazy about Candied Ginger Pieces. They're a tasty snack and good for you—and they clear the sinuses. While munching on a store-bought version, I thought to myself, "I bet I could do this and even better." I bought some fresh gingerroot and brown sugar and went home to try my hand at it. This recipe is spectacular for snacking as well as for sauces. Serve it with the Breaded Salmon Cakes on page 116. It's also good on salads. Save some of the ginger pieces to add to the Oh Nuts! salad on page 167, Ginger Egg or Tofu Scramble on page 220.

3	cups peeled and chopped fresh gingerroot
3	cups water
2	cups packed brown sugar

> In a large saucepan over medium heat, bring the gingerroot, water, and brown sugar to a roiling boil. Boil for 5 minutes. Reduce the heat and simmer for 45 minutes, stirring occasionally. (The longer it cooks, the thicker it gets.)

> Drain the sauce into a bowl and serve.

> You can roll the ginger pieces in sugar, if you like. I prefer them plain. Extra sauce should be stored in an airtight container in the refrigerator.

Yield: About 6 cups

It's easy to make ginger ale, too. Just pour the cooled ginger juice into a tall pitcher and add carbonated water to obtain your desired taste and strength. Pour into a glass and add a lemon wedge, straw, and lots of ice cubes. Refreshing!

Marinara Sauce

This marinara sauce is so very tasty. It's rich with spices and flavor. It's terrific in any meat dish, as well as on vegetables, rice, and noodles. It's definitely one of a kind: the best!

1	tablespoon olive oil
1	cup chopped red onions
2	cloves garlic, diced
3	cups puréed fresh, tomatoes (reserve the juices)
1	cup water
1/4	cup red wine
2	tablespoons tomato paste

1/3	cup packed brown sugar
1	tablespoon dried oregano
1	tablespoon Lawry's lemon pepper
1	teaspoon dried basil
1/2	teaspoon salt
1	teaspoon finely diced fresh thyme
1	teaspoon vanilla extract
1	teaspoon almond extract

> Heat the oil in a small skillet over medium heat, and sauté the onions and garlic until the garlic is lightly browned.

> In a large saucepan over high heat, combine the tomatoes, water, wine, tomato paste, brown sugar, oregano, lemon pepper, basil, salt, thyme, vanilla, and almond extract. Add the sautéed onions and garlic. Bring to a roiling boil.

> Boil for five minutes and reduce the heat to medium low. Cover and simmer for 1 to 2 hours.

> Serve hot with the Pizza Sandwich Loaf on page 158.

> Store any extra sauce in an airtight container in the refrigerator.

Yield: About 2 cups

The tomato is a night-growing plant with fruit that is very rich in vitamin C, A, potassium, and iron. We eat them like candy today, but, according to ar.essortment.com, they weren't even introduced to the United States until the 1800s, when a man named Colonel Robert Gibbon Johnson brought some back with him from a trip overseas. Tomatoes have been proven to help prevent cancer as well as heart disease and even cataracts. One other thing I think is very important is that a couple of nice slices of a juicy, sweet tomato on a sandwich is something to live for!

Orange Shire Dressing

Words are the fashion wardrobe of the mind, revealing its colors and layers of thought. I have to admit the only reason I came up with this sauce is because I love the words orange, shire, and dressing together. They popped into my head one day while I envied a beautiful, but prohibitively expensive, orange blouse. Right there, I created Orange Shire Dressing. Although it sounds snobbish, it's very vitamin C! It's also unusual—which I love.

2	tablespoons olive oil
2	cups plus 1 cup fresh orange juice
1	cup toasted sesame seeds
2	tablespoons butter
1	tablespoon packed brown sugar

1	tablespoon Worcestershire sauce
1	tablespoon fresh lemon juice
1	teaspoon Lawry's lemon pepper
1/8	teaspoon salt
1/8	teaspoon allspice

> In a medium skillet, heat the olive oil over medium heat. Add 1 cup of the orange juice, the sesame seeds, butter, and brown sugar. Bring the mixture to a boil and cook, stirring constantly, until it thickens. Remove from the heat and set aside.

> In a medium bowl, mix the Worcestershire sauce, lemon juice, the remaining 2 cups orange juice, lemon pepper, salt, and allspice with a wire whisk.

> Just before serving, spread a tablespoon of the sesame seed mixture on top of a salad. (If the oil has risen to the top, put this dressing in the microwave for a few seconds until the oil is soft. Then mix well again.) Serve the salad with Orange Shire Dressing on the side.

Yield: About 4 cups

Orange juice provides enormous amounts of vitamin C, making this dressing not only flavorful, but also healthful.

Pesto Sauce

Among the millions of pesto sauces, mine is one of the best! It goes well with veggie sandwiches. It's also the perfect dipping sauce for potato chips and veggies.

5 1/2	ounces fresh basil (about 12 cups)	1	teaspoon cashews
2	cups olive oil	1	tablespoon Lawry's lemon pepper
1	teaspoon pine nuts	1	teaspoon chopped garlic
1	teaspoon almonds	3/4	teaspoon salt
1	teaspoon Candied Walnuts (see page 203)		

> Place the basil, olive oil, pine nuts, almonds, Candied Walnuts, cashews, lemon pepper, garlic, and salt in a blender or food processor. Blend until creamy and the nuts are pulverized.

> Serve with the Garden Patch sandwich on page 106 or the Pesto Egg on page 222.

> Store any extra sauce in an airtight container in the refrigerator.

Yield: About 2 cups

There are two kinds of basil plant: garden and bush. Garden basil, or dried sweet basil, is the most commonly used herb of the two in cooking, though either one can be used. According to botanical.com, in Persia, Malaysia, and Egypt, basil is planted on graves and strewn upon grave sites. Both Greeks and Romans thought the more abuse the plant received, the better it would grow. In Moldavia, it's still believed that a young man will fall in love with a young woman who holds a sprig of basil simply because she holds the tender herb in her hand, making her irresistible. Whatever you believe about basil, it makes a great pesto.

Strawberry Jam Sauce

Here is one of my favorite jam sauces. It's marvelous on buttered toast, meats, and veggies—and as a topping over cake.

2	cups plus 1 cup (about 15 large) fresh, sliced strawberries
1/4	cup honey
1/4	cup white grape juice
1/3	cup spiced rum
2	tablespoons red wine
1	teaspoon fresh lemon juice
	Pinch salt

> In a large skillet over medium heat, combine 2 cups of the strawberries, the honey, grape juice, rum, red wine, lemon juice, and salt. Mix well. Bring to a boil.

> Boil for 3 minutes. Reduce the heat to low and simmer to reduce the liquids (about 10 minutes), stirring frequently.

> When the mixture thickens, remove from the stove, pour it into a bowl. Add the remaining 1 cup strawberries and let cool. Serve over the Fruit Cup on page 246.

> Store any extra sauce in an airtight container in the refrigerator.

Yield: About 1 cup

Peach Jam Sauce

The reason I call this a jam sauce is because it's fabulous on grilled and buttered toast as a jam, as well as on meats and veggies as a sauce. It's also outstanding as a fruit and ice cream topping. One of my favorites.

2	cups plus 1 cup chopped fresh peaches (3 to 4 peaches)
1/4	cup white grape juice
2	tablespoons packed brown sugar
2	tablespoons coffee liqueur

3	tablespoons spiced rum
1	teaspoon lemon juice
1	teaspoon almond extract
	Pinch salt

> In a skillet over medium heat, combine 2 cups of the peaches, the grape juice, brown sugar, coffee liqueur, spiced rum, lemon juice, almond extract, and salt. Mix well and bring to a boil.

> Boil for 3 minutes. Reduce the heat to low and simmer for about 10 minutes, stirring frequently.

> When the mixture thickens, remove from the heat, pour it into a bowl. Add the remaining 1 cup peaches and let it cool slightly before serving.

> Store any extra sauce in an airtight container in the refrigerator.

> Heat the sauce in the microwave before serving.

Yield: 1 1/4 cups

Plum Jam Sauce

This is another jam sauce that is great on grilled and buttered toast as a jam, as well as on meats and veggies as a sauce. This sauce is very rich, so a little goes a long way.

2	cups plus 1 cup peeled, pitted, and chopped plums (about 8 large)
1/3	cup honey
1/2	cup white grape juice
1/3	cup spiced rum

2	tablespoons red wine
1	tablespoon fresh lemon juice
1	tablespoon fresh lime juice
1	teaspoon almond extract
	Pinch salt

> In a skillet over medium heat, combine 2 cups of the plums, the honey, grape juice, spiced rum, red wine, lemon juice, lime juice, almond extract, and salt and mix well. Bring to a boil.

> Boil for 3 minutes. Add the reserved plums, return to a boil, reduce the heat to low, and simmer to reduce the liquid (about 10 minutes), stirring frequently.

> When the mixture thickens, remove from the stove, pour it into a bowl. Add the remaining 1 cup plums and let cool. Serve over the Fruit Cup on page 246.

> Store any extra sauce in an airtight container in the refrigerator.

> When using on meats or veggies, heat the sauce in the microwave before using.

Yield: About 1 cup

Plums are often a forgotten fruit, but they make great jams and sauces. In the summertime, no fruit makes a juicier snack.

Raspberry Jam Sauce

This is another of my rich jam sauces that is fabulous on bread or grilled and buttered toast. It's also delightful on meats and veggies as a sauce or as a cheesecake topping.

2	cups plus 1 cup fresh raspberries		1	teaspoon fresh lime juice
1/4	cup honey		1	teaspoon vanilla extract
2	tablespoons white grape juice			Pinch salt
3	tablespoons spiced rum			

> In a skillet over medium-low heat, combine 2 cups of the raspberries, the honey, grape juice, rum, lime juice, vanilla extract, and salt and mix well. Bring to a boil.

> Boil for 3 minutes. Add the reserved raspberries, return to a boil, reduce the heat to medium low, and simmer to reduce the liquid (about 10 minutes), stirring frequently.

> When the mixture thickens, remove from the heat, pour it into a bowl. Add the remaining 1 cup raspberries and let cool. Serve with the Peanut Butter sandwich on page 110.

> Store any extra sauce in an airtight container in the refrigerator.

Yield: 1 1/2 cups

If you've ever walked past a raspberry bush, then you know that picking a fresh handful and popping them into your mouth is irresistible. For endless summers, I did this in Wisconsin. They're extremely power packed with vitamin C and are loaded with antioxidants. Their season is short; they come and go mighty quickly, so when you see them, grab them and eat them.

Red Wine and Mustard Vinaigrette Dressing

2	cups red wine vinegar
1 1/2	cups deli or spicy brown mustard
1	cup olive oil
3/4	cup packed brown sugar
1	tablespoon Lawry's lemon pepper
1/4	teaspoon salt

> In a large bowl, combine the vinegar, mustard, oil, brown sugar, lemon pepper, and salt and mix well with a wire whisk. Serve with the House Salad on page 168.

> Store any extra dressing in an airtight container in the refrigerator.

> Mix well before each use.

Yield: About 6 cups

According to theepicentre.com, the ancient Greeks believed that the god of healing, Asclepius, was the creator of mustard and gave it to mankind as a gift for its healing properties. Throughout time, mustard has proven its many medicinal qualities, being prescribed for scorpion stings, bee stings, toothaches, snake bites, respiratory problems and much more; however, the oil of mustard, when undiluted, is so powerful that it can actually blister the skin.

Real Apple Butter

Homemade apple butter always seems to be extraordinary. I can't think of any I've ever had I haven't liked.
This is my version, and it's sumptuous over homemade cinnamon ice cream.

1	teaspoon vanilla extract		1/8	teaspoon ground cloves
3	to 4 cups apple cider		1/8	teaspoon allspice
1/2	cup white grape juice		1/8	teaspoon nutmeg
1/4	cup packed brown sugar		12	tart apples, peeled and quartered
1	tablespoon cinnamon			

> In a large skillet over medium heat, combine the vanilla, cider, grape juice, brown sugar, cinnamon, cloves, allspice, and nutmeg. Mix well. Bring to a gentle boil, reduce the heat to low, and simmer for 5 minutes.

> Add the apples. Cover and simmer on low for about 20 minutes.

> Once the apples are very tender, increase the heat to medium and continue cooking, stirring constantly to avoid burning the apples, until the liquid is nearly gone.

> Remove the mixture from the skillet, pour it into a bowl, and let cool for 20 minutes.

> Mix it in a blender or food processor until creamy. Serve on the Garden of Eden sandwich on page 105.

> Store any extra butter in an airtight container in the refrigerator.

Yield: About 8 cups

The health benefits of apples are extensive. Cooking them as long as required in this recipe knocks out some of the nutritional value, but a good deal is still there—and the abundance of flavor will satisfy your sweet tooth.

Real Mint Sauce

This is by far the most stunning mint sauce going!

1 (14-ounce) can sweetened condensed milk
3/4 cup fresh lemon juice
1/2 cup lemon zest

1 tablespoon Lawry's lemon pepper
1/8 teaspoon salt
3 cups finely chopped fresh mint leaves

> In a large bowl combine the milk, lemon juice, lemon zest, lemon pepper, and salt. Mix well.

> Add the mint leaves and mix well. Serve with the lamb sandwich on page 119.

> Store any extra sauce in an airtight container in the refrigerator.

Yield: About 4 cups

Mint is known throughout the world for its cleansing and calming attributes. This sauce can be used on any dish and it, as well as you, will be a hit!

Reuben Sauce

2 cups mayonnaise
1 cup ketchup
1/2 cup piccalilli
1 tablespoon fresh lemon juice

1/2 teaspoon Lawry's lemon pepper
1/8 teaspoon salt

> In a large bowl, combine the mayonnaise, ketchup, piccalilli, lemon juice, lemon pepper, and salt and mix well. Serve with the Reuben sandwich on page 132.

> Store any extra sauce in an airtight container in the refrigerator.

Yield: About 2 cups

Piccalilli is another word for sweet relish. Its main ingredient is the sweet pickle, and it's thought it may be a play on words. That's what we always thought growing up. It's a "fun" word though, and in Chicago, where I grew up, you just didn't have a hot dog without piccalilli and melted cheddar cheese. I still don't!

75

Roasted Red Pepper Sauce

This sauce is delicious, delicious, delicious on any sandwich. I use it often on both fish and veggie sandwiches.

8	Roasted Red Peppers (see page 205)
3	tablespoons half-and-half
1	tablespoon red wine
1	tablespoon Lawry's lemon pepper
1/4	teaspoon salt

> Combine the peppers, half-and-half, wine, lemon pepper, and salt in a blender or food processor. Process until creamy, adding more half-an-half and red wine if necessary. Serve with the Roasted Rumble Bumble on page 128.

> Store any extra sauce in an airtight container in the refrigerator.

> Heat in the microwave before using.

Yield: About 2 cups

I like thick sauces. If you like thinner sauces, add more cream, wine, or both.
Then adjust the spices accordingly.

Spinach Pesto Sauce

This sauce has a unique, hard-to-place flavor. It's the combination of the Candied Walnuts and spinach. Oddly, it gives a bacon-like flavor—and "oddly" is simply delicious!

6	ounces (about 2 cups) fresh spinach
2	cups olive oil
2	tablespoons Candied Walnuts (see page 203)
1	tablespoon Lawry's lemon pepper
1	teaspoon chopped garlic
1/2	teaspoon salt

> Combine the spinach, oil, Candied Walnuts, lemon pepper, garlic, and salt in a blender. Process until creamy. Serve with the Bell Peppers and Onions Sandwich on page 91.

> Store any extra sauce in an airtight container in the refrigerator.

Yield: About 3 cups

Spinach is one of the best sources of iron. Some women are at risk of low iron levels, and spinach is an excellent defense against that condition.

Rosemary-Sage Sauce

Earthy, healthy, heavenly, and very, very rich! This is a wonderful sauce for fish and seafood dishes, and it goes great with lamb, too.

3	tablespoons butter
1/3	cup olive oil
1	(13.5 ounce) can coconut milk
1	teaspoon almond extract
1	teaspoon vanilla extract
1	tablespoon fresh lemon juice

1	tablespoon lemon zest
3	tablespoons finely diced fresh rosemary
3	tablespoons finely diced fresh sage
1/2	tablespoon Lawry's lemon pepper
	Pinch of salt

> In a skillet, melt the butter over medium heat. Add the olive oil, coconut milk, almond extract, vanilla extract, lemon juice, and lemon zest. Stir to mix well. Add the rosemary, sage, lemon pepper, and salt. Mix well and bring to a boil.

> Boil for 3 minutes, stirring constantly. Reduce the heat to low, cover, and simmer for 15 minutes, stirring frequently. Remove the sauce from the stove, pour it into a bowl, and let cool. Serve with the Crab Cakes on page 114.

> Store any extra sauce in an airtight container in the refrigerator.

> This sauce is meant to be served warm, although some people like it as a butter on bread. Heat it in the microwave before using when serving with meats and veggies.

Yield: About 1 1/2 cups

Sweet Red Wine Barbecue Sauce

Barbecue sauce enhances just about any meal and any side dish. I happen to love barbecue sauce as a dip with any snack—it's a great dipping sauce as well as great with all kinds of meats. This is another one of those sauces of which there are a million versions. Be warned that it might be on the spicy side for some people. If you're concerned about that, cut back on the cayenne powder or omit it altogether.

1	cup red wine
1	cup puréed tomatoes
1	cup diced red onions
2	tablespoons tomato paste
1/4	cup molasses
3	tablespoons packed brown sugar

3	tablespoons coffee liqueur
2	tablespoons red wine vinegar
1	tablespoon Lawry's lemon pepper
1 1/2	teaspoons Worcestershire sauce
1	teaspoon salt
1/4	teaspoon cayenne pepper

> In a large saucepan, combine the wine, tomatoes, onions, tomato paste, molasses, brown sugar, coffee liqueur, vinegar, lemon pepper, Worcestershire sauce, salt, and cayenne pepper. Bring to a boil over medium heat. Boil for approximately 5 minutes (watch for splattering), stirring frequently as it thickens.

> Reduce the heat to low, cover, and simmer for about 1 hour, stirring frequently.

> Serve warm with the Barbecued Shrimp sandwich on page 88 and the Rib-Eye Steak sandwich on page 122.

> Store any extra sauce in an airtight container in the refrigerator.

Yield: About 2 1/2 cups

Barbecue sauces have a long rich history. They have evolved over the years, and there are a number of variations to the great sauce. In the eastern Carolinas the sauce dates back to the 1600s, before tomatoes were popular. It consists only of vinegar, salt, black pepper, ground cayenne pepper, and other spices. In the western Carolinas they add small amounts of ketchup, molasses and Worcestershire sauce. In South Carolina the sauce is a unique yellow mustard style of barbecue sauce. Kentucky's barbecue sauce uses a mild tomato base, a "black" sauce, or a peppery hot sauce. The Memphis style brings all three major ingredients together as one: vinegar, tomato, and mustard. Texas covers the gamut of barbecue sauces from thick and spicy with a tomato base to hot peppery thin sauces. Like every other growing trend, there are a few new kids on the block. Florida style barbecue sauce is citrusy and the Hawaiian style barbecue sauce is sweet and sour.

Sweet Horseradish Sauce

One morning around 1:45, about fifteen minutes before I had to get up for work, I bolted up in bed. "Sweet horseradish sauce," I said to myself excitedly and quickly jotted down the ingredients that were darting around in my head. "This is pathetic," I thought. "Most people wake up dreaming about their lover. I wake up dreaming about Sweet Horseradish Sauce!"

2	cups mayonnaise
1/3	cup packed brown sugar
3	tablespoons prepared horseradish

1	tablespoon Lawry's lemon pepper
1/8	teaspoon salt

> In a large bowl, combine the mayonnaise, brown sugar, horseradish, lemon pepper, and salt. Mix well until creamy. Serve this sauce with the Roast Beef sandwich on page 124.

> Store any extra sauce in an airtight container in the refrigerator.

> This sauce is good served warm.

Yield: 1 1/2 cups

An interesting fact about horseradish is that it can relieve indigestion. Any form of radish can do the trick. All radishes are also high in vitamin C, folate, potassium and are low in calories.

Tangy Apricot-Pineapple Sauce

This is one of my most popular sauces—particularly outstanding on Turkey with Tangy Apricot-Pineapple Sauce on Whole Wheat Bread (see page 131). And it's yummy over ice cream, too!

1	cup deli or spicy mustard
3	cups apricot-pineapple preserves

1	tablespoon Lawry's lemon pepper
1/8	teaspoon salt

> Combine the mustard, preserves, lemon pepper, and salt in a large bowl. Mix together very well. Serve on the Turkey sandwich.

> Store any extra sauce in an airtight container in the refrigerator.

Yield: 3 1/2 cups

Nut Butters
(Peanut, Almond, Cashew, or Mixed Nut)

If you or your family are peanut butter and jelly addicts, take a few minutes and make one of these nut butters! You can use the Plum Jam Sauce (see page 69), Raspberry Jam Sauce (see page 70), Real Apple Butter (see page 72), or Strawberry Jam Sauce (see page 67) for heightened flavor.

These recipes are good for any nut butter from pine nut to sunflower seed. I use olive oil, but you can use any oil. Add more or less, depending on your preference for a creamier or thicker nut butter. The amount of salt may need to be adjusted, too. If the oil rises to the top when not in use, stir it into the nut butter, or drizzle it into the sink.

8	ounces unsalted peanuts, almonds, or cashews (if you use salted nuts, reduce the salt to 1/8 teaspoon)

1	to 2 tablespoons olive oil
1/2	teaspoon salt

> Place the nuts in a blender or food processor and blend for about 2 minutes or until the nuts cling to the sides of the machine.

> Turn off the machine and add the oil and salt.

> Turn it on and blend for 1 minute more, or until creamy. (If the mixture seems dry, add a little more oil and process until it's the consistency you like.)

> Store any extra nut butter in an airtight container in the refrigerator.

Yield: About 1 cup

For mixed nut butter, use 2.7 ounces each of peanuts, almonds, and cashews. Increase the oil to 2 to 3 tablespoons, and use the same amount of salt. Remember, some people are allergic to specific nuts. Be sure to disclose which nuts you used.

CHAPTER FOUR

The Best Sandwiches

You may be a little shocked at all the butter I use. While butter is high in fat, according to nutritionist Steven Byrnes, ND, RNCP about 15 percent of the fatty acids in butter are used by vital organs as an energy source rather than stored as fat. So, butter is better, just don't go overboard.

Ingredients make mine the *best* sandwiches in America. It is important to use good, natural ingredients. When you substitute processed and chemically altered ingredients, such as margarine, the sandwiches won't be half as good and won't be as healthy for you. These sandwiches are rich in nutrients, including such vitamins and minerals as A, B6, B12, C, E, K, calcium, copper, fiber, folate, folic acid, iron, niacin (B3), protein, potassium, riboflavin (B2), phosphorus, thiamin, and zinc. Don't let the health factor fool you; they are absolutely full of flavor, too.

Avocado and Melted Swiss on Salsa Bread

2	tablespoons butter
4	slices Salsa Bread (see page 16)
1	cup Guacamole (see page 57)
4	thick slices Swiss cheese
	Lawry's lemon pepper (to taste)
	Salt (to taste)
2	avocados, peeled, pitted and thinly sliced
1	cup Salsa (see page 59)
1	cup mesclun greens (spring mix)
	Berries and grapes for garnish

> Butter both sides of the salsa bread slices and grill until toasted. Cut the bread slices diagonally. Spread the Guacamole Sauce evenly over four of the pieces of bread.

> Put the Swiss cheese in a bowl, sprinkle with lemon pepper and salt, and microwave for about 10 seconds, or until the cheese is melted. Spread the cheese evenly over the Guacamole Sauce.

> Divide the avocado slices between the two sandwiches.

> Drain the Salsa and distribute it over the sandwiches. Add the mesclun greens. Cover with the top slices of grilled bread. Place a toothpick through each section to hold it together.

> Garnish with berries and grapes. Serve with extra Guacamole and Salsa on the side.

Yield: 2 sandwiches

Barbecued Shrimp on Three-Cheese Bread

2	tablespoons plus 4 tablespoons butter
4	slices Three-Cheese Bread (see page 20)
1	cup finely diced red onions
2	pounds jumbo shrimp, peeled, deveined, and chopped
	Lawry's lemon pepper (to taste)

	Salt (to taste)
1	plus 1 cup Sweet Red Wine Barbecue Sauce (see page 81)
1	cup shredded Monterey jack cheese
2	cups mesclun greens (spring mix)
1	cup diced tomatoes
	Berries and grapes for garnish

> Spread 2 tablespoons of the butter on both sides of the bread slices.

> In a skillet, melt the remaining 4 tablespoons of butter over medium heat. Add the red onions and sauté until caramelized (a translucent tan), stirring frequently so they don't burn. Add the shrimp, stirring constantly until thoroughly cooked, about 5 minutes.

> Add the lemon pepper, salt, and 1 cup of the Sweet Red Wine Barbecue Sauce and mix until everything is coated. Add the cheese, cover, and turn off the stove.

> In a skillet or on a griddle, grill the slices of bread on both sides.

> Cut the bread slices diagonally. Divide the shrimp mixture evenly over four of the pieces of bread. Drizzle the remaining 1 cup Sweet Red Wine Barbecue Sauce over the sandwiches. Divide the mesclun greens and tomatoes evenly between the sandwiches. Cover with the top slices of grilled bread, and place a toothpick through each section to hold it together.

> Garnish with berries and grapes.

Yield: 2 sandwiches

Bell Peppers and Onions with Spinach Pesto on Brown Harvest Bread

4	tablespoons plus 2 tablespoons butter
2	red bell peppers, cored, seeded, and julienned
2	yellow bell peppers, cored, seeded, and julienned
2	orange bell peppers, cored, seeded, and julienned
2	green bell peppers, cored, seeded, and julienned
1	large red onion, sliced into rounds
1	tablespoon Lawry's lemon pepper
1/2	teaspoon salt
3/4	cup plus 1/2 cup Spinach Pesto (see page 77)
1	cup shredded Parmesan cheese
4	slices Brown Harvest Bread (see page 46)
2	cups mesclun greens (spring mix)
1	cup chopped tomatoes

> In a skillet, melt 2 tablespoons of the butter over low to medium heat.

> Add the peppers, onion, lemon pepper, and salt and mix. Add 1/2 cup of the Spinach Pesto and mix. Add the Parmesan cheese. Cover and turn the heat to low. The mixture will thicken as it cooks. Cook it until the peppers and onions are cooked to your liking.

> Spread the remaining 4 tablespoons of butter on both sides of the bread slices.

> In a skillet or on a griddle, grill the breads on both sides.

> On a plate, stack two slices of bread and cut them diagonally. On another plate, do the same with the other two slices. Remove the top slices and set aside.

> Divide the pepper mixture evenly between the two sandwiches. Add the mesclun greens and tomatoes. Cover with the top slices of bread and carefully cut the sandwiches diagonally. Place a toothpick through each sandwich section to hold it together.

> Garnish with berries and grapes. Use the remaining pesto for dipping.

Yield: 2 sandwiches

Beef Tenderloin with Coffee Liqueur Mushroom Sauce on French Bread

Beef

1/2	round beef tenderloin (or other beef)
2	tablespoons butter, softened
	Lawry's lemon pepper (to taste)
	Salt (to taste)
1/2	cup coffee liqueur
1	cup water

Sandwich

2	tablespoons plus 2 tablespoons butter
4	slices French bread (see page 27)
	Lawry's lemon pepper (to taste)
	Salt (to taste)
1	cup plus 1 cup Coffee Liqueur Mushroom Sauce (see page 52)
1/4	cup shredded Parmesan cheese
1	cup crumbled baked piecrust

To make the beef:

> Preheat the oven to 350 degrees. In a 12 x 9-inch roasting pan, place the half round of beef. Rub it with the butter. Season with Lawry's lemon pepper and salt.

> Pour the coffee liqueur and water over the beef.

> Cover with aluminum foil and bake for approximately 50 minutes.

To make the sandwich:

> Spread 2 tablespoons of the butter on both sides of the bread slices. Set aside.

> In a skillet, melt the remaining 2 tablespoons of butter over low to medium heat. Add the beef and season with the lemon pepper and salt. Mix well.

> Add 1 cup of Coffee Liqueur Mushroom Sauce and mix well. Add the Parmesan cheese, cover, and turn off the heat.

If you would prefer not to use beef tenderloin, use any beef. For the best sandwich possible, I highly recommend taking the time to prepare the beef according to this recipe. It's all right if the beef comes out a little rare, because it will cook further in the skillet when you heat it.

> In a skillet or on a griddle, grill the slices of bread on both sides.

> On a plate, stack two slices of bread and cut them diagonally. On another plate, do the same with the other two slices. Remove the top slices and set aside.

> Divide the beef mixture among the bottom slices.

> Drizzle the remaining Coffee Liqueuer Mushroom Sauce over the beef.

> Sprinkle the piecrust evenly over the sandwiches, and cover with the top slices of bread. Place a toothpick through each section to hold it together.

> Garnish with berries and grapes.

Yield: 2 sandwiches

Chicken in Creamy Viognier and Pineapple Sauce

18	to 20 chicken tenders
2	tablespoons plus 2 tablespoons butter
2	cups Creamy Viognier and Pineapple Sauce (see page 54)
1	cup shredded Monterey Jack cheese
4	slices White Bread (see page 3) or Honey-Nut Whole Wheat Bread (see page 41)
2	cups mesclun greens (spring mix)
1	cup chopped tomatoes
	Berries
	Grapes

To make the chicken:

> Heat the oven to 375 degrees. Thoroughly clean the chicken with cold water and arrange it in a baking dish. Add water to cover halfway up the chicken. Bake for 18 to 20 minutes, or until completely done. (Cut into the thickest piece: it should be *totally white* throughout with *no* hint of pink or red.)

> Remove the chicken from the oven and let it cool. Chop it into tiny cubes.

To make the sandwich:

> In a skillet, melt 2 tablespoons of the butter over low to medium heat. Add the chicken and Creamy Viognier and Pineapple Sauce and mix.

> Sprinkle the cheese evenly over the chicken mixture, cover, and turn off the heat.

> Spread the remaining 2 tablespoons butter on the slices of bread and grill on both sides.

> On a plate, stack two slices of bread and cut them diagonally. On another plate, do the same with the other two slices. Remove the top slices and set aside.

> Divide the chicken mixture evenly between the two bottom slices of bread.

> Add the mesclun greens and tomatoes. Cover with the top slices of grilled bread. Place a toothpick through each section to hold it together.

> Garnish with some berries and grapes.

Yield: 2 sandwiches

Chicken Salad in Minty Yogurt Sauce on Brown Harvest Bread

4	cups (18 to 20 tenders) cubed cooked chicken		2	tablespoons butter
2	cups Minty Yogurt Sauce (see page 59)		4	slices Brown Harvest Bread (see page 46)
2	cups chopped apples		2	cups mesclun greens (spring mix)
2	cups chopped celery		1	cup chopped tomatoes
1	cup finely chopped Candied Walnuts (see page 203)			

> In a large bowl combine the cooked chicken, Minty Yogurt Sauce, apples, celery, and Candied Walnuts.

> Spread the butter on both sides of the Brown Harvest Bread slices.

> In a skillet or on a griddle, grill the slices of bread on both sides.

> On a plate, stack two slices of the bread and cut them diagonally. On another plate, do the same with the other two slices. Remove the top slices and set aside.

> Divide the chicken mixture evenly onto each bottom slice of bread.

> Divide the mesclun greens and tomatoes among the two sandwiches. Cover with the top slices of bread. Place a toothpick through each section to hold it together.

Yield: 2 sandwiches

Flaked Salmon with Lemon Alive Sauce on Lemon Alive Bread

2	cups fresh spinach
4	tablespoons plus 2 tablespoons butter
1	cup Roasted Pine Nuts (see page 203)
2	pounds boneless, skinless red salmon (tail ends)
	Lawry's lemon pepper (to taste)
	Salt (to taste)

1	cup Lemon Alive Sauce (see page 60)
1	cup shredded Cheddar cheese
4	slices Lemon Alive Bread (see page 8)
2	cups mesclun greens (spring mix)
1	cup chopped tomatoes

> In the microwave cook the spinach and drain it.

> In a skillet melt 4 tablespoons of the butter over low heat. Add the Roasted Pine Nuts. Add the spinach to the skillet.

> After removing the skin from the salmon, place the fish in the skillet. Cover and cook on low for about 5 minutes. Flake apart the salmon with a fork.

> Season with the lemon pepper and salt. Add the Lemon Alive Sauce and mix well.

> Sprinkle the cheese over the salmon, turn off the heat, and cover.

> Spread the remaining 2 tablespoons of butter on both sides of the bread slices and grill them until toasted on both sides.

> On a plate, stack two slices of bread and cut them diagonally. On another plate, do the same with the other two slices. Remove the top slices and set aside.

> Divide the salmon mixture evenly among the bottom slices of bread.

> Divide the mesclun greens and tomatoes between the sandwiches. Cover with the top slices of bread. Place a toothpick through each section to hold it together.

Yield: 2 sandwiches

Curried Chicken on Spicy White Pepper-Jack Bread (aka the "O" Special)

4	cups (18 to 20 tenders) cubed cooked chicken
2	cups Curry Sauce (see page 51)
2	cups shredded carrots
1	cup chopped Roasted Almonds (see page 203)

2	tablespoons butter
4	slices Spicy White Pepper-Jack Bread (see page 19)
2	cups mesclun greens (spring mix)
1	cup chopped tomatoes

> In a large bowl combine the chicken, Curry Sauce, carrots, and almonds.

> Spread the Butter on both sides of the Spicy White Pepper-Jack Bread slices.

> In a skillet or on a griddle, grill the bread on both sides.

> On a plate, stack two slices of bread and cut them diagonally. On another plate, do the same with the other two slices. Remove the top slices and set aside.

> Divide the chicken mixture evenly between the two bottom slices of bread.

> Divide the mesclun greens and tomatoes over the sandwiches. Cover with the top slices of bread. Place a toothpick through each section to hold it together.

Yield: 2 sandwiches

Lovely Lavender

When I was five, I was good friends with a little red-haired boy with lots of freckles. His name was Billy Lonigro. We delighted in running and playing in a huge field between our homes. We couldn't run too long because Billy tired easily, so instead we'd lie on our backs, the hot sun making us lazy. The tall grass waved in the wind, and we'd make pictures out of the clouds. Purple flowers on long greens stems covered the field. They smelled so good! Billy picked one, handed it to me and said, "I love you." I giggled and told him I loved him, too. As time went by, Billy became more and more easily exhausted. Sometimes he couldn't play at all. I missed him terribly. One day, Billy's sister came to the house crying. She told me Billy had died. I wasn't sure what that meant, but she told me we'd never see Billy again. He didn't make it to six years old. He died of leukemia. Just the same, every time I went to the field where the long green stems with purple flowers grew, I picked one, smelled it, and told Billy I loved and missed him. Years later, I learned its name: lavender. It became one of my lifelong favorite flowers, colors, and herbs.

Flaked Salmon with Lavender Mint Love Sauce on Lavender Mint Love Bread

2	tablespoons plus 2 tablespoons butter
1/2	red onion, sliced into rounds
2	pounds boneless, skinless red salmon (tail ends)
	Lawry's lemon pepper (to taste)
	Salt (to taste)
1	cup Lavender Mint Love Sauce (see page 58) plus extra for serving

1	cup shredded manchego cheese
4	slices Lavender Mint Love Bread (see page 7)
2	cups mesclun greens (spring mix)
1	cup chopped tomatoes

> In a skillet, melt 2 tablespoons of the butter over low heat. Add the onion and cook until soft.

> After removing the skin and gray under-skin of the salmon, place the fish in the skillet. Cover and let it cook on low for about 5 minutes. Flake apart the salmon with a fork.

> Season with the lemon pepper and salt. Add the Lavender Mint Love Sauce, and mix well.

> Sprinkle the cheese over the salmon, turn off the heat, and cover.

> Spread the remaining 2 tablespoons of butter on both sides of the bread slices and grill them until toasted on both sides.

> On a plate, stack two slices of bread and cut diagonally. On another plate, do the same with the other two slices. Remove the top slices and set aside.

> Divide the salmon mixture over the bottom slices of bread.

> Divide the mesclun greens and tomatoes over the sandwiches. Cover with the top slices of grilled bread. Place a toothpick through each section to hold it together.

> Serve with a side of Lavender Mint Love Sauce.

Yield: 2 sandwiches

Garden of Eden on Concord Grape Bread

This sandwich is absolutely heavenly; hence, the name!

1	apple, peeled and thinly sliced
1/2	papaya, peeled, seeded and thinly sliced
1	banana, thinly sliced
1	kiwifruit, peeled and thinly sliced
2	tablespoons butter
4	slices Concord Grape Bread (see page 23)
1	cup Nut Butter of your choice (see page 83)
1	cup Real Apple Butter (see page 72)
1	cup manchego cheese
2	cups mesclun greens (spring mix)

> Prepare the fruits and divide them between two plates. (Cover and refrigerate if not using immediately.)

> Spread the butter on both sides of the Concord Grape Bread.

> In a skillet or on a griddle, grill the bread on both sides.

> On a plate, stack two slices of bread and cut them diagonally. On another plate, do the same with the other two slices. Remove the top slices and set aside.

> Spread the Nut Butter evenly over the bottom slices, followed by the Real Apple Butter.

> Sprinkle the manchego cheese over the sandwiches.

> Layer the fruits onto the sandwiches beginning with the apple, then papaya, banana, and kiwi.

> Divide the mesclun greens between the sandwiches. Cover with the top slices of grilled bread. Place a toothpick through each section to hold it together.

Yield: 2 sandwiches

The fruits in this bread are seasonal and sometimes may be hard to find. Feel free to substitute whatever fruit is in season in your area. The point is to load up on fruits and be creative.

Garden Patch with Creamy Candied Carrot Sauce on Maple Merlot Bread

2	tablespoons plus 2 tablespoons butter
1	zucchini, sliced into 8 rounds
1/2	cucumber, sliced into 8 rounds
1/2	red onion, diced
4	slices Maple Merlot Bread (see page 28)
1	cup Creamy Candied Carrot Sauce (see page 53)

1	cup shredded manchego cheese
2	cups shredded carrots
1	cup sliced black olives
2	avocados, peeled, pitted, and each sliced in 8 pieces
2	cup mesclun greens (spring mix)
1	cup chopped tomatoes

> In a skillet, melt 2 tablespoons of the butter over low heat.

> Add the zucchini, cucumbers, and red onion. Let simmer on low until soft. Transfer to a plate.

> Spread the remaining 2 tablespoons of butter on both sides of the bread.

> In a skillet or on a griddle, grill both sides of the bread.

> On a plate, stack two slices of bread and cut them diagonally. On another plate, do the same with the other two slices. Remove the top slices and set aside.

> Divide the Creamy Candied Carrot Sauce evenly between the bottom slices of bread.

> Sprinkle the manchego cheese over the sauce.

> Divide the carrots, olives, and avocados between the sandwiches.

> Layer the zucchini mixture over each sandwich.

> Divide the mesclun greens and tomatoes between them.

> Drizzle any remaining Creamy Candied Carrot Sauce over each. Cover with the top slices of bread. Place a toothpick through each section to hold it together.

Yield: 2 sandwiches

Grilled Cheese on White Bread

The extraordinary bread raises this sandwich far above the usual "grilled cheese on white". That being said, feel free to use any of the breads in this book for a grilled cheese sandwich. There's no going wrong. I typically use three different cheeses. Use your favorites!

1 cup shredded manchego cheese	4 plus 4 tablespoons butter
1 cup shredded sharp Cheddar cheese	4 slices Basic White Bread
1 cup shredded Parmesan cheese	(see page 3)

> Mix the cheeses in a large bowl.

> In a skillet (or two skillets if they're small), melt 4 tablespoons of the butter over low heat.

> Spread the remaining 4 tablespoons butter on both sides of the bread slices.

> Lightly grill the bread slices, just to heat up, and remove the top slices, leaving the bottom slices in the pan. Turn over the bottom slices and grill the other side.

> Divide the cheese mixture over both slices in the pan.

> Place the top slice of bread on top of the cheese, with the grilled side against the cheese. Cover and keep the heat low.

> Check for desired doneness by gently lifting the sandwich with a spatula. Flip the sandwiches when ready and cover. When grilled to desired degree of doneness, slide the sandwiches onto plates. Let cool for a few minutes and carefully slice diagonally.

Yield: 2 sandwiches

Grilled Peanut Butter and Raspberry Jam with Potato Chips on French Bread

This sandwich is great on any of the breads in this book, but it's also outstanding on the Concord Grape Bread.

4   plus 4 tablespoons butter

4   slices French Bread (see page 27) or Concord Grape Bread (see page 23)

1   cup Peanut Butter (see page 83)

1   cup Raspberry Jam Sauce (see page 70)

2   cups crushed potato chips

> Spread 4 tablespoons of the butter evenly on both sides of the bread slices. On a plate, stack two slices of bread. Do the same thing on another plate with the other two slices. Remove the top slices and set aside.

> Divide the Peanut Butter between the bottom slices. Do the same with the Raspberry Jam.

> Cover the sandwiches with the top slices of bread.

> In a skillet (or two), melt the remaining 4 tablespoons of butter, cook the sandwiches over low heat, covered.

> After a few minutes, check the bottom of the sandwiches for desired doneness. Flip the sandwiches.

> When done, slide the sandwiches onto the plates. Carefully slice the sandwiches.

> Lift the top slices off, put 1 cup of the potato chips on each sandwich, and replace the top slice.

> Serve with any remaining potato chips.

Yield: 2 sandwiches

Herb Grain Breaded Fish Sandwich with Lemon Alive Sauce on Lemon Alive Bread

One of my sisters loves salmon on sandwiches. My mom likes halibut. I prefer cod sandwiches. Choose your favorite fish, but be certain it's washed well and boned.

2	fish fillets (your favorite), cleaned
1/2	cup whole wheat flour seasoned with Lawry's lemon pepper and salt (to taste)
1	egg, beaten with 2 tablespoons water
1	cup Herb Grain Breading (see page 204)
6	tablespoons plus 2 tablespoons butter

2	slices Cheddar cheese
4	slices Lemon Alive Bread (see page 8)
1	cup Lemon Alive Sauce (see page 60)
2	cups mesclun greens (spring mix)
1	cup chopped tomatoes

> Dredge the fish fillets in the seasoned flour and then dip in the beaten egg mixture.

> Coat the fillets with the Herb Grain Breading.

> In a large skillet over medium-low heat, melt 6 tablespoons of the butter. Add the breaded fish fillets.

> When the fillets are brown, about 5 minutes, turn and cook the other side. When done, cover each fillet with a slice of cheese. Cover the skillet and turn the heat to low.

> Spread the remaining 2 tablespoons butter on both sides of the bread slices.

> In a skillet or on a griddle, grill the bread on both sides.

> Place one slice of bread on each of two plates.

> Place one of the fish fillets on each slice.

> Drizzle 1/2 cup of the Lemon Alive Sauce over each sandwich.

> Place half the mesclun greens and half the tomatoes on each fillet. Cover with the top slices of bread and carefully cut diagonally.

Yield: 2 sandwiches

Herb Grain Breaded Crab Cakes with Rosemary-Sage Sauce on Rosemary-Sage Bread

This recipe is easier than it looks! I just want to make sure it's as understandable as possible. It's well worth the reading and making.

2 1/2	servings instant mashed potato granules
2	cups fresh or canned crabmeat
1/2	cup finely diced celery
1/4	cup finely diced red onion
1/4	cup finely diced fresh basil
2	tablespoons butter, melted
1	teaspoon fresh lemon juice
1	teaspoon lemon zest
1	teaspoon Lawry's lemon pepper
1/4	teaspoon dill weed
1/2	cup whole wheat flour seasoned with salt and lemon pepper

1	egg
2	tablespoons water
1	cup Herb Grain Breading (see page 204)
6	tablespoons plus 2 tablespoons butter
2	slices Monterey Jack cheese
4	slices Rosemary-Sage Bread, white (see page 15) or wheat (see page 42)
1	cup Rosemary-Sage Sauce (see page 78)
2	cups mesclun greens (spring mix)
1	cup chopped tomatoes

> In a large bowl, combine the potatoes, crabmeat, celery, onion, basil, butter, lemon juice, lemon zest, lemon pepper, and dill weed. Mix very well with your hands. Form the mixture into two large patties.

> Coat the patties with the seasoned flour.

> Beat together the egg and water together to make an egg wash. Immerse the patties in the egg wash.

> Coat the patties with the Herb Grain Breading.

> In a medium skillet, melt 6 tablespoons of the butter over medium-low heat until bubbly.

> Gently fry the patties until they're toasty brown on both sides and the insides are hot. Place a slice of Monterey Jack cheese on each patty. Keep the heat low and cover the skillet.

> While the patties are cooking, spread the remaining 2 tablespoons of butter on both sides of the bread slices.

> In another skillet or on a griddle, grill the bread slices on both sides.

> On each of two plates, place a bread slice. Place a patty on each slice.

> Drizzle ½ cup of the Rosemary-Sage Sauce over each patty.

> Cover each with half the mesclun greens and half the tomatoes.

> Cover with the top slice of bread and carefully cut diagonally.

Yield: 2 sandwiches

Herb Grain Breaded Salmon Cakes with Ginger Sauce on Ginger-Goat Cheese Whole Wheat Bread

Salmon Cakes

2	cups skinless, boneless salmon (fresh or canned), flaked
2 1/2	cups instant potato granules
1/2	cup finely diced celery
1/2	cup finely diced red onion
1/2	cup finely diced green bell pepper
1/4	cup crumbled goat cheese
1	cup plus 2 tablespoons Ginger Sauce (see page 61)
1	teaspoon Lawry's lemon pepper
1/2	teaspoon salt
1/2	cup whole wheat flour seasoned with lemon pepper and salt
1	egg
2	tablespoons water
1	cup Herb Grain Breading (see page 204)
6	plus 2 tablespoons butter
4	slices Ginger-Goat Cheese Whole Wheat Bread (see page 38)
2	cups mesclun greens (spring mix)
1	cup chopped tomatoes

> In a large bowl, combine the potato granules, salmon, celery, onion, green bell pepper, goat cheese, 2 tablespoons of the Ginger Sauce, lemon pepper, and salt. Mix very well with your hands.

> Form the salmon mixture into two patties. Coat the patties in the seasoned flour.

> Beat together the egg and water to make an egg wash. Coat the patties in the egg wash and then the Herb Grain Breading.

> In a skillet, melt 6 tablespoons of the butter over medium-low heat.

> Add the patties and cook until toasty brown on one side. Flip and cook until toasty brown on the other side. Reduce the heat to low and cover.

> Spread the remaining 2 tablespoons butter on both sides of the bread slices.

> In a skillet or on a griddle, grill the bread on both sides.

> Put one slice of the bread on each of two plates, and set aside the top slices.

> Place a patty on each bottom slice.

> Drizzle the remaining 1 cup of the Ginger Sauce over the patties (1/2 cup each patty).

> Cover each with half the mesclun greens and half the tomatoes.

> Cover with the top slices and cut them diagonally.

Yield: 2 sandwiches

Lamb with Real Mint Sauce
on Roasted Red Pepper-Brie-Mint Bread

Lamb

3	pounds leg of lamb
1	cup red wine
1	cup water
1	teaspoon Lawry's lemon pepper plus some for seasoning the lamb
	Salt (to taste)

Sandwich

4	plus 2 tablespoons butter
1	cup roasted pine nuts (see page 203)

1	cup diced red onions
1	cup roasted red peppers (see page 205)
1/4	teaspoon salt
1	cup chopped brie cheese
4	slices Roasted Red Pepper Brie Mint Bread (see page 12)
1	cup Real Mint Sauce (see page 75)
2	cups mesclun greens (spring mix)
1	cup chopped tomatoes

To roast the lamb:

> Preheat the oven to 350 degrees. Clean the lamb under cold running water, and place it in a 12 x 9-inch roasting pan. Add the wine, water, and Lawry's lemon pepper and salt.

> Cover the pan with aluminum foil and cook for 2 to 2 1/2 hours.

> Remove the lamb from the oven, take off the foil, and let it cool. Cut enough lamb to equal 4 cups.

For the sandwich:

> In a skillet, melt 4 tablespoons of the butter on low.

> Add 4 cups lamb, pine nuts, onions, red peppers, 1 teaspoon lemon pepper, salt and mix.

> Add the cheese and cover. Keep the heat low.

> Spread the remaining 2 tablespoons butter on both sides of the bread slices.

> In a skillet or on a griddle, grill both sides of the bread.

> On a plate, stack two slices of bread and cut them diagonally. On another plate, do the same with the other two slices. Remove the top slices and set aside.

> Divide the lamb mixture evenly over the two bottom slices. Then drizzle the Real Mint Sauce over the lamb, and divide the mesclun greens and tomatoes over them. Cover with the top slices of bread. Place a toothpick through each section to hold it together.

Yield: 2 sandwiches

TBLT (Turkey Bacon, Lettuce, and Tomato) on Horseradish Parmesan Bread

This sandwich is wonderful on any bread. Originally, I paired it with French Bread (see page 27), but it's even more delicious on Horseradish Parmesan Bread (see page 4).

16	slices turkey bacon		2	cups mesclun greens (spring mix) or lettuce
2	tablespoons butter		1	cup chopped tomatoes
4	slices Horseradish Parmesan Bread			
1/4	cup mayonnaise			

> In a skillet, cook the turkey bacon to desired crispness.

> Spread the butter on both sides of the bread slices.

> In a skillet or on a griddle, grill the bread on both sides.

> On a plate, stack two slices of bread and cut them diagonally. On another plate, do the same with the other two slices. Remove the top slices and set aside.

> Spread the mayonnaise evenly over the bottom slices.

> Place 4 slices of turkey bacon on each sandwich half.

> Divide the mesclun greens and tomatoes over the sandwiches, and cover with the top slices. Place a toothpick through each section to hold it together.

Yield: 2 sandwiches

Red Deviled Egg Salad Sandwich on Spicy White Pepper-Jack Bread

10	hard-boiled eggs, separated
1 1/2	cups mayonnaise
1	tablespoon ketchup
1/2	cup shredded Monterey Jack cheese
1	teaspoon Lawry's lemon pepper
1/4	teaspoon salt
1/4	teaspoon cayenne
1	cup chopped celery

1/2	cup Roasted Red Peppers (see page 205)
2	tablespoons butter
4	slices Spicy White Pepper-Jack Bread (see page 19)
2	cups mesclun greens (spring mix)
1	cup chopped tomatoes

> In a large bowl combine the egg yolks with the mayonnaise, ketchup, Monterey jack cheese, lemon pepper, salt, and cayenne. By hand or with an electric mixer, mix everything until smooth and creamy.

> Add the egg whites, celery, and roasted red peppers and mix well.

> Spread the butter on both sides of the bread slices.

> In a skillet or on a griddle, grill both sides of the bread.

> On a plate, stack two slices of bread and cut them diagonally. On another plate, do the same with the other two slices. Remove the top slices of bread and set aside.

> Scoop one-quarter of the egg salad onto each sandwich half, and divide the mesclun greens and tomatoes over the egg salad.

> Place a toothpick through each section to hold it together.

Yield: 2 sandwiches

Rib-Eye Steak with Sweet Red Wine Barbecue Sauce on French Bread

6	plus 2 tablespoons butter
2	cups sliced mushrooms
1	cup diced red onions
4	rib-eye steaks, chopped into bite-sized pieces
	Lawry's lemon pepper (to taste)
	Salt (to taste)

1/2	cup plus 1 1/2 cups Sweet Red Wine Barbecue Sauce (see page 81)
1	cup shredded mozzarella cheese
4	slices French Bread (see page 27)
2	cups mesclun greens (spring mix)
1	cup chopped tomatoes

> In a skillet, melt 6 tablespoons of the butter over medium heat.

> Add the mushrooms and onions and cook until the mushrooms are dark brown and the onions are caramelized (a translucent tan).

> Add the steak and reduce the heat to medium low.

> Add the lemon pepper and salt. Add 1/2 cup of the Sweet Red Wine Barbecue Sauce and mix. Cook to degree of doneness.

> Sprinkle the mozzarella cheese over the meat. Cover and turn off the heat.

> Spread the remaining 2 tablespoons butter on both sides of the bread slices and grill them until toasted on both sides.

> On a plate, stack two slices of bread and cut them diagonally. On another plate, do the same with the other two slices. Remove the top slices and set aside.

> Divide the steak evenly over the bottom slices and drizzle the remaining 1 1/2 cups Sweet Red Wine Barbecue Sauce on top.

> Spread the mesclun greens and tomatoes over the sandwiches. Cover with the top slices. Place a toothpick through each section to hold it together.

Yield: 2 sandwiches

Roast Beef with Sweet Horseradish Sauce on Horseradish Parmesan Bread

Roast Beef

5	pounds rib roast, rolled or standing
1	cup orange juice
1	cup water
	Lemon pepper and salt (to taste)

Sandwich

4	tablespoons plus 4 tablespoons butter
4	cups chopped or torn roast beef

	Lawry's lemon pepper (to taste)
	Salt (to taste)
4	thick slices Swiss cheese
4	slices Horseradish Parmesan Bread (see page 4)
1	cup Sweet Horseradish Sauce (see page 82)
2	cups mesclun greens (spring mix)
1	cup chopped tomatoes

For the roast beef:

> Preheat the oven to 300 degrees.

> Wash the roast under cold, running water. Place it in a 12 x 9-inch roasting pan.

> Add the orange juice, water, and lemon pepper and salt.

> Bake, uncovered, for 1 1/2 to 2 hours or about 35 minutes per pound. Baste as needed.

> When finished, remove from oven and let cool. Cut enough roast beef to equal 4 cups (for 2 sandwiches). You can chop the roast beef, or tear it. Store the extra in an airtight container in the refrigerator or freezer.

For the sandwich:

> In a skillet, melt 4 tablespoons of the butter over low heat.

> Add the roast beef, lemon pepper, and salt, and mix well.

> In the pan, separate the roast beef into two portions, and cover each one with 2 slices of Swiss cheese. Cover and keep the heat low.

> Spread the remaining butter on both sides of the bread slices.

> In a skillet or on a griddle, grill both sides of the bread.

> On a plate, stack two slices of bread and cut them diagonally. On another plate, do the same with the other two slices. Remove the top slices and set aside.

> Spread 1/2 cup of the Sweet Horseradish Sauce evenly on the bottom slices, reserving the rest.

> Scoop one portion of the roast beef onto each sandwich, and add the remaining Sweet Horseradish Sauce.

> Divide the mesclun greens and tomatoes over the sandwiches.

> Add the top slices and cut the sandwiches diagonally. Place a toothpick through each section to hold it together.

Yield: 2 sandwiches

Turkey Bacon with Cream Cheese and Apple Butter on Cinnamon-Raisin Bread

16	slices turkey bacon
2	tablespoons butter
4	slices Cinnamon-Raisin Bread (see page 30)
8	tablespoons cream cheese
8	tablespoons Real Apple Butter (see page 72)

> In a skillet, cook the turkey bacon to desired crispness.

> Spread the butter on both sides of the bread slices.

> In a skillet or on a griddle, grill the breads on both sides.

> On a plate, stack two slices of bread and cut them diagonally. On another plate, do the same with the other two slices. Remove the top slices and set aside.

> Spread two tablespoons of cream cheese on each sandwich half.

> Spread the Real Apple Butter on each.

> Arrange 4 slices of turkey bacon on each sandwich half, and cover with the top slices of bread. Place a toothpick through each section to hold it together.

Yield: 2 sandwiches

Roasted Rumble Bumble with Roasted Red Pepper Sauce on Honey-Nut Wheat Bread

1	cup Roasted Red Peppers (see page 205)
1	cup broccoli florets
1	cup sliced carrots (in rounds)
1	cup sliced zucchini (in rounds)
1	cup sliced mushrooms
1	cup sliced red onions (in rounds)
1	cup chopped asparagus spears
2	tablespoons plus 1/2 teaspoon olive oil
1	tablespoon Lawry's lemon pepper
1	teaspoon salt

1	cup chopped fresh, beets
2	tablespoons Butter
4	slices Honey-Nut Whole Wheat Bread (see page 41)
3/4	cup plus 1/4 cup Roasted Red Pepper Sauce (see page 76)
1/2	cup plus 1/2 cup goat cheese
2	cups mesclun greens (spring mix)
1	cup chopped tomatoes
1	teaspoon sweet dried basil
1	teaspoon dill weed

> Preheat the oven to 375 degrees.

> On a baking sheet, arrange the Roasted Red Peppers, broccoli, carrots, zucchini, mushrooms, onions, and asparagus, and cover them with 2 tablespoons of the olive oil, lemon pepper, and salt.

> Mix well so that all the veggies are oiled. Use more oil, if needed.

> Roast for about 20 minutes, stirring every five minutes or so.

> When the veggies are done, remove them from the oven and separate into two portions on the baking sheet.

> In a small skillet, heat 1/2 teaspoon of olive oil over medium heat and cook the beets until tender. (They're cooked separately to avoid discoloring other foods.)

> Spread the butter on both sides of the bread slices.

> In a skillet or on a griddle, grill the bread on both sides.

> On a plate, stack two slices and cut them diagonally. On another plate, do the same thing with the other two slices. Remove the top slices and set aside.

> Spread ¼ cup of the Roasted Red Pepper Sauce on the bottom slices and then ½ cup of the goat cheese on the sauce.

> With a spatula, scoop one portion of the roasted veggies onto each sandwich.

> Drizzle the remaining Roasted Red Pepper Sauce over them.

> Divide the mesclun greens and tomatoes over the sandwiches. Cover with the top slices of bread. Place a toothpick through each section to hold it together.

Yield: 2 sandwiches

Turkey with Tangy Apricot-Pineapple Sauce on Whole Wheat Bread

6	tablespoons plus 2 tablespoons butter		4	slices Whole Wheat Bread (see page 34)
4	cups sliced, chopped, or torn cooked turkey (leftover or good deli)		1	cup plus 1/2 cup Tangy Apricot-Pineapple Sauce (see page 82)
	Lawry's lemon pepper (to taste)		2	cups mesclun greens (spring mix)
	Salt (to taste)		1	cup chopped tomatoes
4	thick slices Swiss cheese			

> In a skillet, melt 6 tablespoons of the butter on low heat.

> Add the turkey, lemon pepper, and salt, and mix.

> Separate the turkey into four portions in the skillet, top each portion with a slice of cheese, cover, and keep the heat low.

> Spread the remaining butter on both sides of the bread slices.

> In a skillet or on a griddle, grill the breads on both sides.

> On a plate, stack two slices of bread and cut them diagonally. Do the same with the other two slices. Remove the top slices and set aside.

> Drizzle 1/4 cup of the Tangy Apricot-Pineapple Sauce on each sandwich half.

> With a spatula, scoop one portion of the turkey and Swiss onto each half.

> Drizzle the remaining Tangy 1 cup Apricot-Pineapple Sauce over the sandwiches.

> Divide the mesclun greens and tomatoes between the sandwiches, and cover with the top slices. Place a toothpick through each section to hold it together.

Yield: 2 sandwiches

Reuben with Reuben Sauce on Herbed Rye Bread

2	to 3 pounds corned beef
2	(12-ounce) cans beer
12	ounces water
	Lawry's lemon pepper (to taste)
	Salt (to taste)
4	tablespoons plus 2 tablespoons butter
1	cup diced red onions
1/2	cup diced fresh beets
4	cups cooked, thinly sliced or chopped corned beef

2	cups sauerkraut, thoroughly drained (wring it in a cheesecloth or towel and set it in a strainer until ready to use)
	Lawry's lemon pepper (to taste)
	Salt (to taste)
4	thick slices Swiss cheese
4	slices Rye Bread (see page 45)
1	cup plus 1 cup Reuben Sauce (see page 75)

For the corned beef:

> Preheat the oven to 350 degrees. Wash the corned beef under cold running water, and place it in a 12 x 9-inch roasting pan. Add the beer, water, lemon pepper, and salt.

> Cover with aluminum foil and cook approximately 1 1/2 to 2 hours.

> Remove from the oven and take off the foil.

> Slice or chop enough corned beef to make 4 cups.

For the sandwich:

> In a skillet, melt 4 tablespoons of the butter on low.

> Add the onions and beets, and cook until the onions are caramelized (a translucent tan).

> Add the corned beef, sauerkraut, lemon pepper, and salt, and mix.

> Divide the corned beef mixture into two portions in the pan.

> Place 2 slices of cheese over each portion and cover. Turn off the heat.

> Spread the remaining butter on both sides of the bread slices and grill them on both sides until toasted.

> On a plate, stack two slices of bread and cut them diagonally. On another plate, do the same with the other two slices. Remove the top slices and set aside.

> Spread 1 cup of the Reuben Sauce over the bottom slices.

> With a spatula, slide one portion of the corned beef mixture over the sauce on each sandwich. Spread the remaining Reuben Sauce over each. Cover with the top slices. Place a toothpick through each section to hold it together.

Yield: 2 sandwiches

Tuna Salad on Rye

4	cups white albacore tuna
1	cup sweet relish (piccalilli)
1/2	cup mayonnaise
1	cup shredded carrots
1/2	cup chopped celery
2	tablespoons packed brown sugar

2	tablespoons butter
4	slices Rye Bread (see page 45)
4	tablespoons Candied Walnuts (see page 203)
2	cups mesclun greens (spring mix)
1	cup chopped tomatoes

> In a large bowl, combine the tuna, sweet relish, mayonnaise, carrots, celery, and brown sugar.

> Spread the butter on both sides of the bread slices.

> In a skillet or on a griddle, grill the bread on both sides.

> On a plate, stack two slices of bread and cut them diagonally. Do the same with the other two slices. Remove the top slices and set aside.

> Scoop 1/4 of the tuna mixture onto each sandwich half and then add the Candied Walnuts.

> Divide the mesclun greens and tomatoes between the sandwiches. Cover with the top slices of bread. Place a toothpick through each section to hold it together.

Yield: 2 sandwiches

A few years ago, I dated a palate-challenged man whose evening dinners consisted solely of white rice and ground turkey. That's all! After a few discussions about the monotonous fare, I made a bet (for a pair of amethyst earrings) that I could prepare the best meal he'd ever tasted. If I failed, I'd never again try to alter his culinary preferences. I made a loaf of wheat bread and bought a juicy turkey breast from the store, ripped it into bite-sized bits, and tossed it in a skillet with butter, lemon pepper, and salt. Once the meat was warm, I melted Swiss cheese over it. I grilled the breads so that they were crispy outside, but soft inside. Knowing his love for apricot jam, I used it as the base for the sauce I created, and then added the sauce to the meat and melted Swiss. That evening I assembled our sandwiches and presented them in the dining room. The next day when I got home, the sweetest card and a little box with a gold ribbon awaited me: beautiful amethyst earrings.

Turkey Salad on Rye

When I was growing up, my parents would make a turkey for Thanksgiving and Christmas. Those were the only two times of the year turkey was prepared at home. After the holiday feasts, the leftover turkey would become turkey salad sandwiches or hot turkey sandwiches with hot gravy. One of my brothers or my father would flip on the television, and we'd eat turkey and watch football games all day long. Those are great memories for me.

4	cups chopped cooked turkey (from the deli or leftovers)		2	tablespoons honey
1	cup chopped celery		1	tablespoon mustard seeds
1	cup cooked snow peas		1	tablespoon Lawry's lemon pepper
1	cup finely diced red onions		1	teaspoon salt
1	cup shredded carrots		2	cups mesclun greens (spring mix)
1	cup Monterey Jack cheese (optional)		1	cup chopped tomatoes
1/2	cup raisins (optional)		2	tablespoons butter
1	cup mayonnaise (more if you prefer)		4	slices Rye bread (see page 45)

> In a large mixing bowl, combine the turkey, celery, snow peas, onions, carrots, cheese, raisins, mayonnaise, honey, mustard seeds, lemon pepper, and salt. Make sure the mixture is thoroughly combined.

> Spread the butter on both sides of the bread and grill to desired crispness.

> Cut the bread slices diagonally and divide four of the slices between two plates, setting aside the top four slices.

> On the bottom slices place 1 cup of the turkey mixture.

> Divide the spring mix evenly between the two sandwiches, and do the same with the tomatoes.

> Cover with the top slices of bread and place a toothpick through each sandwich section to hold together.

Yield: 2 sandwiches

Peanut Butter, Honey, and Caramelized Bananas on Brown Harvest Bread

This is the sandwich I told you about earlier that my "angel" friend likes, only I took the liberty of adding caramelized bananas to the sandwich. It's fabulous without the bananas, too, but, I love bananas with it, and I'm sure my angel friend won't mind my adding them.

2   plus 4 tablespoons butter

2   bananas, peeled and quartered

4   slices Brown Harvest Bread
     (see page 46)

1/2   plus 1/2 cup honey

1   cup Nut Butter (see page 83)

> Melt 2 tablespoons of the butter in a skillet over medium-low heat.

> Add the banana and cook until the sugars are caramelized.

> Toast the bread and spread the remaining 3 tablespoons butter on top of all four slices. Cut the bread slices diagonally.

> For a softer bread spread 1/2 cup of the honey onto two of the bread slices and then spread with the Nut Butter. (The honey will melt into the warm bread.) For a crispier sandwich, spread the Nut Butter on first and then the honey.

> Divide the banana quarters between the sandwiches.

> Spread the remaining 1/2 cup honey on the remaining two slices of bread. Place on top of the bananas to make a sandwich.

> Garnish with some fresh berries.

Yield: 2 sandwiches

Acorn Squash in Herb Grain Breading with Goat Cheese on Whole Wheat Bread

Acorn squash is, in my opinion, one of the best squashes out there. Having one of the naturally sweetest flavors of the squash family, acorn squash has always been one of my mother's favorites. See page 209 for an acorn squash side dish that's delicious and page 189 for Autumn Squash Soup.

1	acorn squash		4	slices Whole Wheat Bread (see page 34)
1/2	cup whole wheat flour seasoned with lemon pepper and salt		4	tablespoons goat cheese
			4	tablespoons Ginger Sauce (see page 61)
2	to 3 eggs, beaten		2	cups mesclun greens (spring mix)
1	cup Herb Grain Breading (see page 204)		1	cup chopped tomatoes
8	plus 2 tablespoons butter or olive oil			

> Cook the squash in the microwave for 10 to 15 minutes, or until almost cooked through. You want it done but firm enough to cut.

> Let the squash cool for several minutes and then cut it into 4 thick slices. Slice the outer skin away from the squash and clean away the seeds.

> Roll each slice of squash in the whole wheat flour mixture in the bowl, the beaten eggs, and then the Herb Grain Breading.

> In a skillet, melt 8 tablespoons of the butter (or heat 8 tablespoons of olive oil) over medium-low heat.

> Cook the squash pieces in the skillet until toasty brown on each side.

> Toast the bread slices and spread the remaining 2 tablespoons butter on both sides of each piece of bread. Slice the bread diagonally.

Remove the top slices of bread and put off to the side.

> Divide the squash among the bottom slices.

> Divide the goat cheese between the sandwiches, over the squash slices.

> Drizzle the ginger sauce evenly over each sandwich.

> Divide the mesclun spring greens and tomatoes between the sandwiches.

> Cover with the top slices of bread and place a toothpick through each sandwich section to hold together.

> Garnish with fresh berries and grapes.

Yield: 2 sandwiches

Open-Face Eggplant Parmesan on French Bread

8	plus 2 tablespoons butter (plus extra for the skillet as needed)
	Lawry's lemon pepper (to taste)
	Salt (to taste)
8	thick slices eggplant, peeled
1	to 1/2 cups flour
2	cups shredded Parmesan cheese
2	cups Marinara Sauce (see page 62)
4	slices French Bread (see page 27)

> Melt 8 tablespoons of the butter in a skillet over medium-low heat.

> Add the lemon pepper and salt and mix well.

> Roll the eggplant in flour and add to the skillet. Cook until soft and browned, turning and adding more butter if needed.

> Sprinkle 1/4 cup of Parmesan cheese on top of each slice of eggplant. Cover with a lid and turn off the heat.

> Heat the Marinara Sauce in a saucepan over medium heat or in a microwave.

> Spread the remaining 2 tablespoons of butter on both sides of the slices of bread and grill until toasted.

> Divide the bread between two plates and place two pieces of eggplant on top of each slice.

> Pour the hot Marinara Sauce over the eggplant and sprinkle with a little more Parmesan cheese.

Yield: 2 sandwiches

My Favorite Hot Dog

When I was a little girl, my father used to take me to the White Sox baseball games at Comiskey Park in Chicago, Illinois. He was a total White Sox fan. He was also a die-hard Cubs fan, as was (and still am) I, and Wrigley Field, also in Chicago, was where we caught the Cubs games. Well, anybody who has ever been to a ball game knows that you have to eat a hot dog or two while you're there. It's religion! There's no way around it. I've even known vegetarians who concede to eating hot dogs at the ball games. It's a must, AND . . . they're the most awful things you'll ever eat! Still, my memories of hot dogs begin with great times at the ball games with my father. Now, Chicago has some of the greatest hot dog joints in the world! No lie! The recipe I'm giving you is, except for the bun, my all-time favorite hot dog recipe. Oh, it's pretty standard, but SOOOO good!

My Favorite Hot Dog

3	ounces English Muffin dough (see page 24)
4	plus 2 tablespoons butter
2	cups finely chopped red onions
2	cups shredded sharp Cheddar cheese

2	all-beef hot dogs
	Celery salt (to taste)
1	cup sweet relish
1	cup chopped tomatoes
	Ketchup and mustard (to taste)

> Divide the English Muffin dough into two sections and roll out each section as long as a hot dog bun. Keep them thin because they'll rise on the grill.

> Grill the dough in a skillet over medium-low heat until well browned on both sides, about 20 minutes. Flip as needed to avoid burning. When they are browned, slice them open and butter and grill the inside.

> In a skillet, melt 2 tablespoons of the butter over medium heat.

> Add the onions and sauté until caramelized.

> Add the cheese and turn off the heat.

> Place the hot dogs in a saucepan with enough water to cover. Bring to a roiling boil over high heat. Turn off the heat and remove the hot dogs.

> In a skillet, melt the remaining 4 tablespoons of butter over medium-low heat. Slice the hot dogs down the middle and sauté in the butter.

> Place the English Muffin hot dog buns on two plates. Place the hot dogs in the buns sliced side up. Divide the cheese and onion mixture into two portions and pour into the hot dogs.

> Sprinkle with desired amount of celery salt. Divide the sweet relish and tomatoes between the hot dogs.

> Add desired amounts of ketchup and mustard.

> Serve with potato chips.

Yield: 2 sandwiches

Stuffed Broccoli and Cheddar Cheese English Muffins

This couldn't be easier to make and is an instant hit with everyone who eats it!

4	tablespoons plus 2 tablespoons butter
4	cups fresh broccoli florets
	Lawry's lemon pepper (to taste)
	Salt (to taste)
4	English Muffin halves (see page 24)
2	cups shredded Cheddar cheese

> In a skillet, melt 4 tablespoons of the butter over medium-low heat.

> Add the broccoli, lemon pepper, and salt.

> Cover and cook to desired degree of doneness.

> Butter and grill, or toast and butter, the muffin halves.

> Sprinkle the Cheddar cheese over the broccoli, cover, and reduce the heat to low.

> Put 2 muffin halves on separate plates, and set the other two aside.

> Divide the broccoli mixture into two portions, and slide each portion onto one of the muffin halves. Top with the other halves.

Yield: 2 sandwiches

Stuffed Mushroom, Onion, and Jack English Muffin

4	tablespoons plus 2 tablespoons butter		Salt (to taste)
2	cups diced red onions	2	cups shredded Monterey jack cheese
4	cups sliced mushrooms	4	English Muffin halves (see page 24)
	Lawry's lemon pepper (to taste)		

> In a skillet, melt 4 tablespoons of the butter over medium-low heat.

> Add the onions, mushrooms, lemon pepper, and salt.

> Turn the heat to high and cook until the mushrooms are a crispy deep brown (or to your preference) and the onions are caramelized (a translucent tan). Stir continually to prevent burning.

> Sprinkle the cheese over the mixture, cover, and reduce the heat to low.

> Toast the English muffin halves and spread the remaining 2 tablespoons butter on top.

> Put 2 muffin halves on separate plates, and set the other two aside.

> Divide the mushroom mixture into two portions, and slide each portion onto one of the muffin halves. Cover with the top muffins.

Yield: 2 sandwiches

Stuffed Spinach and Swiss English Muffin

4	tablespoons plus 2 tablespoons butter
6	cups fresh spinach
	Lawry's lemon pepper (to taste)
	Salt (to taste)
2	cups shredded Swiss cheese
4	English Muffin halves (see page 24)

> In a skillet, melt 4 tablespoons of the butter over medium heat.

> Add the spinach and cook thoroughly. (Because spinach holds high volumes of water, drain it well once it's cooked.)

> Add the lemon pepper and salt and mix well.

> Sprinkle the Swiss cheese over the spinach, cover, and reduce the heat low.

> Toast the English muffin halves and spread the remaining 2 tablespoons butter on top.

> Put two muffin halves on separate plates, and set the other two aside.

> Divide the spinach mixture into two portions, and slide each portion onto one of the muffin halves. Cover with the top muffin.

Yield: 2 sandwiches

Stuffed Strawberry, Granola, Cream Cheese, and Brown Sugar English Muffins (aka "The Greg")

Greg came into the cafe every day, but rarely greeted me with a hello. Instead it was, "I'm hungry, but I don't know what I'm in the mood for. Something different. You're the creative one; create something!" He loved my English Muffins, so I invented this quick and easy number for him.

4	plus 2 tablespoons butter
4	cups sliced fresh, strawberries
2	cups cream cheese
4	tablespoons packed brown sugar
4	cups Granola (see page 223)
4	English Muffin halves (see page 24)

> In a skillet, melt 4 tablespoons of the butter over medium-low heat.

> Add the strawberries, cream cheese, and brown sugar, and mix well.

> Add the granola and mix.

> Reduce the heat to low and cover.

> Toast the English muffin halves and spread the remaining 2 tablespoons butter on top.

> Put two muffin halves on separate plates, and set the other two aside.

> Divide the granola mixture into two portions, and slide each portion onto one of the muffin halves. Cover with the top muffin.

Yield: 2 sandwiches

CHAPTER FIVE

Sandwich Loaves

The Sweet Dough recipe (see page 17) is fabulous for making what I call sandwich loaves. Sandwich loaves are wonderful for parties and a great way to make a sandwich in a form that can feed many people. Bake the sandwich fillings directly into the bread and avoid making each sandwich separately. They're very popular and very tasty. Portion the Sweet Dough into two sections (batches), and let it come to room temperature before baking. Read on for some of my favorite recipes, but remember, you can create your own, too, with your favorite fillings!

Mixed Garden Sandwich Loaf

2	tablespoons plus 2 tablespoons butter
1	cup chopped zucchini
1	cup chopped broccoli
1	cup chopped mushrooms
1	cup chopped red onions
1	cup shredded carrots
1	tablespoon Lawry's lemon pepper (or to taste)
1	teaspoon salt (or to taste)
1	batch Sweet Dough (see page 17)
2	tablespoons olive oil

1	tablespoon dill weed
1	cup diced fresh basil
2	cups shredded Cheddar cheese
6	cups fresh spinach
2	cups Roasted Pine Nuts (see page 203)
1	cup shredded Monterey Jack cheese
1	egg
2	tablespoons water
2	tablespoons sesame seeds

> In a skillet, melt 2 tablespoons of the butter over medium-low heat.

> Add the zucchini, broccoli, mushrooms, red onions, and carrots.

> Season with lemon pepper and salt to taste. Mix well and cover.

> Roll out the Sweet Dough so that the long side is perpendicular to your body. The dough should be only slightly thicker than paper thin. Spread the olive oil over the dough.

> Sprinkle 1 tablespoon of the lemon pepper, 1 teaspoon of the salt, the dill weed, basil, Cheddar cheese, spinach, and Roasted Pine Nuts over the rolled dough.

> Distribute the sautéed veggies over the Roasted Pine Nuts and the Monterey Jack cheese over the veggies.

> Season with a little more lemon pepper and salt.

> Generously butter a large baking sheet.

> Preheat the oven to 375 degrees.

> With your hands, tightly roll the dough into a loaf, with the rolling action going away from your body. To hold in most of the fillings, fold the outer edges of the dough as you roll. Place the loaf onto the prepared sheet seam side down.

> Beat together the egg and water to make an egg wash. Brush the egg wash over the dough and sprinkle with sesame seeds.

> Bake for 40 to 45 minutes.

> Remove the loaf from the oven and let it cool 30 minutes before slicing.

> To serve, arrange a mound of mesclun greens and a thick slice of sandwich loaf on a plate, and garnish with a slice of watermelon.

Yield: 10 to 12 servings

Green Garden Sandwich Loaf

2	plus 2 tablespoons butter		2	tablespoons olive oil
1	cup diced celery		1	cup Pesto Sauce (see page 66)
1	cup diced broccoli		1	tablespoon chopped fresh dill weed
1	cup diced green bell pepper		1	tablespoon chopped fresh lavender
1	cup diced kale		1	tablespoon chopped fresh mint
4	cups fresh spinach		1	cup chopped fresh basil
1	cup diced Swiss chard		2	cups plus 1 cup crumbled goat cheese
	Lawry's lemon pepper (to taste)		1	egg
	Salt (to taste)		2	tablespoons water
1	batch Sweet Dough (see page 17)		2	tablespoons sesame seeds

> In a skillet, melt 2 tablespoons of the butter over medium-low heat.

> Add the celery, broccoli, bell pepper, kale, spinach, Swiss chard, lemon pepper, and salt. Mix well and cover.

> Roll out the Sweet Dough so that the long side is perpendicular to your body. The dough should be only slightly thicker than paper thin. With your hands, spread the olive oil and Pesto Sauce over the dough.

> Sprinkle additional lemon pepper and salt, as well as the dill weed, lavender, mint, and basil evenly over the sauce.

> Spread the spinach mixture and 2 cups of the goat cheese over the spices.

> Distribute the sautéed veggies, then the remaining goat cheese on top.

> Season with a little more lemon pepper and salt.

> Preheat the oven to 375 degrees.

> Generously butter a large baking sheet.

> With your hands, tightly roll the dough into a loaf, with the rolling action going away from your body. To hold in most of the fillings, fold the outer edges of the dough as you roll. Place the loaf onto the prepared sheet seam side down.

> Beat together the egg and water to make an egg wash. Brush the egg wash over the dough and sprinkle with the sesame seeds.

> Bake for 40 to 45 minutes.

> Remove the loaf from the oven, and let it cool for 30 minutes before slicing.

> To serve, arrange a mound of mesclun greens and a thick slice of sandwich loaf on a plate and garnish with sliced avocado and a few berries.

Yield: 10 to 12 servings

Manchego, Broccoli, Chicken Sandwich Loaf

2	plus 2 tablespoons butter
4	cups diced chicken tenders
1	tablespoon Lawry's lemon pepper (or to taste)
1	teaspoon salt (or to taste)
3	cups broccoli florets

1	batch Sweet Dough (page 17)
2	tablespoons olive oil
1	tablespoon sweet dried basil
2	cups plus 1 cup manchego cheese
	Juice of 1 lemon

> In a large skillet, melt 2 tablespoons of the butter over medium-low heat.

> Add the chicken tenders, lemon pepper, and salt. Mix well and cover. Cook, stirring occasionally, for about 15 minutes, or until cooked through.

> In another large skillet, melt the remaining 2 tablespoons butter over low heat. Add the broccoli and more lemon pepper and salt to taste. Mix well and cover.

> Roll out the Sweet Dough so that the long side is perpendicular to your body. The dough should be only slightly thicker than paper thin. Spread the olive oil over the dough.

> Sprinkle more lemon pepper and salt, as well as the basil, onto the dough.

> Spread 2 cups of the cheese over the basil.

> Add the chicken to the pan with the broccoli and mix well.

> Spread the mixture over the dough and add the remaining cheese.

> Sprinkle the lemon juice over the cheese.

> Preheat the oven to 375 degrees.

> Generously butter a large baking sheet.

> With your hands, tightly roll the dough into a loaf, with the rolling action going away from your body. To hold in most of the fillings, fold the outer edges of the dough as you roll. Place the loaf onto the prepared baking sheet seam side down.

> Bake for 40 to 45 minutes.

> Remove the loaf from the oven and let it cool 30 minutes before slicing.

> To serve, arrange a mound of mesclun greens and a thick slice of sandwich loaf on a plate, and garnish with a slice of watermelon.

Yield: 10 to 12 servings

Turkey and Wild Rice Sandwich Loaf

3	tablespoons plus 2 tablespoons butter
3	cups chopped cooked turkey
2	cups prepared long grain-wild rice blend
1	tablespoon Lawry's lemon pepper (or to taste)
1/2	teaspoon salt (or to taste)
2	cups shredded Cheddar cheese
1	batch Sweet Dough (see page 17)
2	tablespoons olive oil
1	egg
2	tablespoons water

> In a skillet, melt 2 tablespoons of the butter over medium-low heat.

> Add the turkey, prepared rice, and lemon pepper and salt to taste. Mix well.

> Add 1 cup of the Cheddar cheese and cover. (Don't *cook* these ingredients because they're already cooked. Just warm them.) Mix and turn off the heat.

> Roll out the Sweet Dough so that the long side is perpendicular to your body. The dough should be only slightly thicker than paper thin. With your hands, spread the olive oil over the dough.

> Sprinkle the tablespoon of lemon pepper and the 1/2 teaspoon of salt evenly over the dough. Add the remaining Cheddar cheese.

> Distribute the turkey and rice mixture over the cheese.

> Drizzle with the remaining 3 tablespoons butter.

> Preheat the oven to 375 degrees.

> Generously butter a large baking sheet.

> With your hands, tightly roll the dough into a loaf, with the rolling action going away from your body. To hold in most of the fillings, fold the outer edges of the dough as you roll. Place the loaf onto the prepared sheet seam side down.

> Beat together the egg and water to make an egg wash. Brush the egg wash over the dough.

> Bake for 40 to 45 minutes.

> Remove the loaf from the oven and let it cool 30 minutes before slicing.

> To serve, arrange a mound of mesclun greens on a plate and a thick slice of the sandwich loaf on the greens. Garnish with fresh berries.

Yield: 10 to 12 servings

Pizza Sandwich Loaf

2	tablespoons butter
2	pounds ground beef, crumbled
1	teaspoon plus 1 teaspoon salt
1	teaspoon plus 1 teaspoon oregano
1	teaspoon allspice
1 1/2	cups Marinara Sauce (see page 62) plus extra for serving

1	batch Sweet Dough (see page 17)
2	tablespoons olive oil
3 3/4	cups shredded mozzarella cheese plus extra for serving

> In a skillet, melt the butter over medium heat and add the ground beef, 1 teaspoon of the salt, 1 teaspoon of the oregano, and the allspice. Mix well.

> Add 1 1/2 cups of the Marinara Sauce and mix. Reduce the heat to low, and cover.

> Roll out the Sweet Dough so that the long side is perpendicular to your body. The dough should be only slightly thicker than paper thin. With your hands, spread the olive oil over the dough.

> Sprinkle the remaining salt, oregano, and 3 cups of the mozzarella cheese over the dough.

> Mix the meat and spices in the skillet well, and distribute the mixture evenly over the cheese.

> Sprinkle the remaining mozzarella cheese over the meat.

> Preheat the oven to 375 degrees.

> Generously butter a large baking sheet.

> With your hands, tightly roll the dough into a loaf, with the rolling action going away from

your body. To hold in most of the fillings, fold the outer edges of the dough as you roll. Place the loaf onto the prepared sheet seam side down.

> Bake for 40 to 45 minutes.

> Remove the loaf from the oven and sprinkle 3/4 cup of the mozzarella cheese over the top.

> Return it to the oven for ten minutes or until the cheese melts.

> Remove the loaf from the oven and let it cool for 30 minutes.

> To serve, spread 1/4 cup of the Marinara Sauce and any leftover meat on a plate. Place a thick slice of the Pizza Sandwich Loaf on top. Sprinkle mozzarella cheese around the plate. Top the slice with more Marinara Sauce. Serve with a cool, crisp side salad (see page 163).

Yield: 10 to 12 servings

Cream Cheese, Chives, and Lox Sandwich Loaf

Although this isn't your authentic lox and bagel, it is extremely delicious. Whenever you go to your favorite deli to buy lox, get two to three pounds. You will need that much to make this absolutely delectable sandwich loaf.

2	(16-ounce) containers cream cheese, at room temperature	1	batch Sweet Dough (see page 17)
3	tablespoons spiced rum	2	tablespoons olive oil
1	teaspoon brown sugar	2	to 3 pounds lox
	Half-and-half (as needed)	5	tablespoons butter, melted, plus extra for serving
2	cups finely diced fresh chives	1	egg, beaten
	Lawry's lemon pepper (to taste)	2	tablespoons water
	Salt (to taste)		

> In a large mixing bowl, combine the cream cheese, spiced rum, and brown sugar. With an electric mixer running, add half-and-half to obtain a spreadable consistency.

> Add the chives, lemon pepper, and salt and, with a spoon, combine with the cream cheese mixture.

> Preheat the oven to 375 degrees.

> Roll out the dough until it's almost paper thin.

> Spread the olive oil over the dough. Add more lemon pepper and salt to taste evenly over the dough.

> Spread the cheese mixture evenly over the dough.

> Arrange the lox in rows evenly over the dough.

> Drizzle 3 tablespoons of the butter evenly over the lox.

> Very carefully, tightly roll the dough into a loaf, rolling away from your body with the seam of the dough ending up on the bottom of the loaf. Fold in the edges to hold in the ingredients.

> Grease a large baking sheet with the remaining 2 tablespoons of butter.

> Slide the loaf onto the greased baking sheet.

> Beat together the egg and water to make an egg wash. Brush the egg over the dough.

> Bake for 40 to 45 minutes.

> Remove from the oven and let cool 30 minutes before slicing.

> Serve with a side of melted butter.

Yield: 10 to 12 servings

When serving, cut thick slices, arrange on a mound of spring mix on a plate, and garnish with some fresh berries. Serve with a side of piping hot Lentil Soup (see page 196) or a cool, crisp side salad (see page 163).

Eggplant Parmesan Sandwich Loaf

I've yet to make this Eggplant Parmesan Sandwich Loaf and not get rave reviews for its outstanding flavor. This is one of the most flavor-packed sandwiches I make. It can easily become one of those snacks that arouses you from your sleep, drawing you into the kitchen at one in the morning.

6	plus 2 tablespoons butter
8	cups chopped eggplant
	Lawry's lemon pepper (to taste)
	Salt (to taste)
2	cups grilled sliced onions (optional)
2	tablespoons olive oil

1	plus 1 cup Marinara Sauce (see page 62)
2	plus 2 cups shredded Parmesan cheese
1	batch Sweet dough (see page 17)
1	egg, beaten
2	tablespoons water

> In a skillet, melt 6 tablespoons of butter over medium-low heat.

> Add the eggplant and turn to coat the eggplant with butter.

> Add the lemon pepper and salt and mix very well.

> Cook the eggplant for several minutes, stirring as needed to avoid burning. Add the onions if using. When you can easily slide a fork through the eggplant, remove the pan from the heat.

> Roll out the dough until it's almost paper thin.

> Preheat the oven to 375 degrees.

> Spread the olive oil evenly over the dough.

> Spread 1 cup of the Sweet Marinara Sauce evenly over the dough.

> Sprinkle 2 cups of the shredded Parmesan cheese evenly over the sauce on the dough.

> Remove the skillet from the stove and distribute the eggplant mixture evenly over the sauce and cheese.

> Sprinkle the remaining Parmesan cheese over the eggplant mixture.

> Drizzle the remaining Marinara Sauce over the top of the mixture.

> Very carefully, tightly roll the dough into a loaf, rolling away from your body with the seam of the dough ending up on the bottom of the loaf. Fold in the edges to hold in the ingredients.

> With the remaining 2 tablespoons of butter, grease a large baking sheet.

> Slide the Eggplant Parmesan Sandwich Loaf onto the greased baking sheet.

> Beat together the egg and water to make an egg wash. Brush the egg wash over the dough. Spread any oozing sauce over the top of the loaf.

> Sprinkle some Parmesan cheese on top of the loaf.

> Bake for 40 to 45 minutes.

> Remove from the oven and let cool for 30 minutes before slicing.

Yield: 10 to 12 servings

Tuna Melt Sandwich Loaf

This Tuna Melt Loaf is so simple to make and kids love it just as much as adults. The sandwich is, in my opinion, best served warm or at room temperature. However, it's also good, and easy to pack, as a lunch.

6	cups washed, very well drained white albacore tuna	2	tablespoons olive oil
1	cup mayonnaise	2	plus 2 cups shredded Cheddar cheese
1	cup sweet relish	5	tablespoons butter, melted
1	teaspoon salt	1	egg, beaten
1	batch Sweet Dough (see page 17)	2	tablespoons water

> In a large mixing bowl, combine the tuna, mayonnaise, sweet relish, and salt. Mix very well.

> Preheat the oven to 375 degrees.

> Roll out the dough until it's almost paper thin.

> Spread the olive oil evenly over the dough.

> Sprinkle 2 cups of the Cheddar cheese evenly over the dough.

> Spread the tuna mixture evenly over the Cheddar cheese.

> Sprinkle the remaining 2 cups of shredded Cheddar cheese over the tuna mixture.

> Drizzle 3 tablespoons of butter evenly over the mixture.

> Very carefully, tightly roll the dough into a loaf, rolling away from your body with the seam of the dough ending up on the bottom of the loaf. Fold in the edges to hold in the ingredients

> Grease a large baking sheet with the remaining 2 tablespoons butter.

> Slide the loaf onto the greased baking sheet.

> Beat together the egg and water to make an egg wash. Brush the egg wash over the dough.

> Bake for 40 to 45 minutes.

> Remove from the oven and let cool for 30 minutes before slicing.

Yield: 10 to 12 servings

When serving, cut into thick slices, arrange on a mound of spring greens on a plate, and garnish with some fresh berries. Serve with a cool, crisp, side salad (see page 163).

CHAPTER SIX

Salads

Read on to enhance any of the marvelous sandwiches
in this book with a fabulous salad. These salads can be
easily adapted for one, if you're dining alone, or twenty,
if you're throwing a bash. They're easy to prepare, rich
in fiber and nutrition, and they taste wonderful.

The Red Wine and Mustard Vinaigrette (see page
71) and the Orange Shire Dressing (see page 65) were
made specifically for these salads.

Enjoy!

Kandra's Salad

This salad is a piece of art! I created it for a friend who asked me daily to make her a "special salad." She wanted something different every time. Finally, I combined a number of ingredients and named it after her. Here's Kandra's special salad.

3	tablespoons butter
1	cucumber, cut lengthwise into eighths
2	zucchini, cut lengthwise into fourths
2	cups sliced mushrooms
4	cups mesclun greens (spring mix)
2	cups chopped tomatoes

2	cups shredded carrots
2	cups chopped black olives
1	cup shredded manchego cheese
1	cup Roasted Almonds (see page 203)
1	avocado, peeled, pitted, and sliced (4 slices per half)

> In a skillet, melt the butter over medium-low heat and add the cucumbers and zucchini. Cook until hot but still crisp. Remove and set aside. Add 1 cup of the mushrooms to the skillet and cook until they're dark brown.

> Divide the mesclun greens between two large dinner salad bowls.

> On one side of each salad place 1/2 cup of tomatoes. Directly across from them, place another 1/2 cup of tomatoes.

> Between the tomatoes arrange 1/2 cup of the shredded carrots. Directly across from them arrange another 1/2 cup of carrots.

> Spread the remaining mushrooms and 1 cup of the black olives over the center of each.

> Between the carrots and the tomatoes place two cucumber slices and two zucchini slices. Place two more cucumbers and zucchini directly across from them.

> Sprinkle 1/2 cup of the manchego cheese over the salad.

> Sprinkle 1/2 cup of the Roasted Almonds over the cheese.

> Form a star in the center of each salad with 4 avocado pieces

> Serve with a side of Red Wine and Mustard Vinaigrette Dressing (see page 71) or Orange Shire dressing (see page 65) and a slice of the grilled bread of your choice.

Yield: 2 salads

Oh Nuts!

Most people I know snack on nuts or sprinkle nuts on their salads and desserts. But what would it be like to make nuts the main feature of a salad? This salad is spectacular! The ginger pieces and ginger sauce make it a knockout!

2	cups cashews
2	cups almonds
2	cups pine nuts
1/3	cup olive oil
	Salt (optional)
2	tablespoons plus 2 tablespoons butter
1/4	cup packed brown sugar
1	to 2 tablespoons honey

2	cups walnuts
4	zucchini, cut lengthwise in fourths
4	cups mesclun greens (spring mix)
2	cups chopped tomatoes
2	cups shredded carrots
1	cup crumbled goat cheese
1/2	cup ginger pieces (see page 61)
2	servings Ginger Sauce (see page 61)

> Preheat the oven to 400 degrees. To roast the cashews, almonds, and pine nuts, place them on a baking sheet, drizzle with the olive oil, and put some oil in your hands. Mix the nuts around to coat them. Sprinkle them with salt, if desired. Cook for 10 to 15 minutes or to desired crispness and color.

> To candy the walnuts, in a skillet melt 2 tablespoons butter. Add the brown sugar, honey, and salt. Mix well until creamy. Add the walnuts and coat well. Remove from the heat when done.

> To prepare the zucchini, in a skillet melt the remaining 2 tablespoons butter over medium-low heat and add the zucchini. Cook until hot but still crisp.

> In four large dinner salad bowls (each serving one), evenly divide the mesclun greens.

> In the center of each salad, divide the tomatoes and the carrots.

> Arrange 4 of the zucchini slices like a star in the middle of each salad.

> Within the star shape of *each* salad, add 1/2 cup of each type of nuts: cashews, almonds, pine nuts, and walnuts.

> Divide the goat cheese and ginger pieces among the salads.

> Serve with Ginger Sauce and a slice of the grilled bread of your choice.

Yield: 4 salads

House Salad

I call this House Salad because it's basic and so simple to pre-
pare. It's great either as an accompaniment to a sandwich or
soup or on its own.

4	cups mesclun greens (spring mix)
2	cups shredded carrots
2	cups chopped tomatoes
1	cup chopped red onions
1	cup shredded Monterey Jack cheese
1	cup Roasted Almonds (see page 203)

> Divide the mesclun greens evenly between two salad bowls, then sprinkle on the carrots, tomatoes, onions, cheese, and Roasted Almonds.

> Serve with a side of Red Wine and Mustard Vinaigrette Dressing (see page 71) or Orange Shire Dressing (see page 65) and a slice of grilled bread of your choice.

Yield: 2 salads

Spinach Salad

Spinach salads have always been popular and are vitamin-and-iron packed. Here's my version—simple, elegant, and tasty.

4	cups fresh spinach
4	hard-boiled eggs, sliced
2	cups chopped tomatoes
2	cups shredded carrots
1	cup Candied Walnuts (see page 203)
1	cup shredded Parmesan cheese
1	cucumber, cut lengthwise into eighths

> Divide the spinach evenly between two large dinner salad bowls.

> On one side of each bowl, arrange 1/2 cup of the tomatoes. Directly across from them, arrange another 1/2 cup of tomatoes.

> On one side of the bowl, arrange 1/2 cup of the carrots. Directly across from them, arrange another 1/2 cup of carrots.

> Between the carrots and tomatoes, arrange 2 of the sliced hard-boiled eggs.

> In the center of each salad, form a star (having an open center) with 4 of the cucumber slices.

> In the center of each star, arrange 1/2 cup of the Candied Walnuts.

> Sprinkle 1/2 cup of the Parmesan cheese over the salad.

> Serve with the Red Wine Mustard Vinaigrette Dressing (see page 71), the Orange Shire Dressing (see page 65), or the Ginger Sauce (see page 61), as well as a slice of the grilled bread of your choice.

Yield: 2 salads

Mixed Berry Salad

This is really a summer salad but can be served any time of year. Use fresh berries when possible. Frozen berries don't quite fill the bill, but they'll do. You can substitute other fruits if you like, such as cranberries for the golden raspberries.

4	cups mesclun greens (spring mix)
1	cup blackberries
1	cup red raspberries
1	cup blueberries
1	cup golden raspberries
2	bananas, peeled and cut into 16 rounds each

2	strawberries
2	dollops vanilla yogurt
2	chocolate kisses
2	slices Peanut Butter Chocolate Fudge Bread, buttered and grilled (see page 11)
1	cup Plum Jam Sauce (see page 69)

> Divide the mesclun greens between two salad bowls.

> For each salad and in this order arrange around the side of the bowl 1/2 cup of the blackberries, 1/2 cup of the red raspberries, 1/2 cup of the blueberries, and 1/2 cup of the golden raspberries.

> Between the berries place four slices of banana (sixteen slices for each salad).

> Slice the strawberries into quarters, leaving them intact by not slicing all the way through. Place the strawberries in the middle of the salads with the sliced part up so they gently fall apart to make a "flower."

> Place a dollop of vanilla yogurt in the center of the strawberries and a chocolate kiss in the center of the yogurt.

> Butter and grill two slices of Peanut Butter Chocolate Fudge bread.

> Serve with a side of warmed Plum Jam Sauce and a slice of Peanut Butter Chocolate Fudge bread.

Yield: 2 salads

Peaches, Pears, and Cottage Cheese

This salad is an absolute favorite with a meal, for a light lunch, or a snack. Many people use canned fruits with this salad, but it is best with fresh fruits.

2	large crispy leaves of Romaine lettuce, washed
1	ripe peach
1	ripe pear
2	cups cottage cheese

2	dashes salt
1	cup Peach Jam Sauce (see page 68)
2	slices Roasted Red Pepper Brie Mint Bread (see page 12)

> Place a Romaine lettuce leaf on each of two salad plates.

> Peel the fruit if desired. Cut the peach and pear into halves and core each half. Place a pear half and a peach half on opposites sides of each plate.

> Spoon 1/2 cup of cottage cheese inside each fruit half.

> Sprinkle a little salt on top.

> Serve with 1/2 cup of warmed Peach Jam Sauce and a slice of buttered and grilled Roasted Red Pepper Brie Mint Bread on the side.

Yield: 2 salads

Hot German Potato Salad with Turkey Bacon

8	medium red potatoes, peeled and quartered
16	slices turkey bacon
4	tablespoons butter
2	cups sliced medium-size mushrooms
1	medium red onion, finely diced
1	large celery stalk, thinly sliced
2	cups cooked fresh spinach leaves, well drained

2	tablespoons flour
3/4	cup water
3/4	cup apple cider vinegar
1/2	cup brown sugar (packed)
2	teaspoons lemon pepper
1/2	teaspoon salt

> In a large pot combine the potatoes with enough water to cover. Bring to a boil over medium-high heat and cook for about 15 minutes.

> In a skillet over medium heat, cook the turkey bacon to desired crispness and then transfer to a plate.

> In the same skillet, melt the butter over medium heat and add the mushrooms and onion. Cook until they are caramelized, about 8 minutes.

> Add the celery and cooked spinach.

> Add the flour and mix very well.

> Add the water, vinegar, brown sugar, lemon pepper, and salt and mix well.

> Increase the heat to medium high, bring to a boil, and allow to thicken, about 10 minutes, stirring as needed to avoid clumping.

> Add the turkey bacon and mix well.

> Drain the potatoes and transfer them to a large mixing bowl.

> While the potatoes are still hot, pour the bacon and vegetable mixture over them and gently mix well to make sure all the potatoes are covered with the sauce.

Yield: 8 servings

Though this is "hot" German potato salad, it can be served cold, too.

Spinach Salad with Ten Beans and Cheddar Cheese

This salad is very healthy; it's a great source of dietary fiber. It can be served as a complete meal or as a side salad along with an entrée. I use Cheddar cheese, but you can use any cheese. This is a very filling salad, so you don't need large portions, especially if you're serving it with an entree. Since it takes a while to prepare the bean mix, you may want to do that a day ahead.

1   (16-ounce) package 10-bean mix
6   cups fresh spinach
     Lawry's lemon pepper (to taste)
     Salt (to taste)
2   cups melted Cheddar cheese
2   Roma tomatoes, quartered
     Red Wine and Mustard Vinaigrette Dressing (see page 71)

> Prepare the bean mix according to the package directions.

> Divide the spinach between two salad plates.

> On top of the spinach, place 1 cup of the prepared beans.

> Season with the lemon pepper and salt.

> Divide the Cheddar cheese and the tomatoes between the salads.

> Serve with a side of Red Wine and Mustard Vinaigrette Dressing.

Yield: 2 salads

Beets with Eggs, Grilled Onions and Goat Cheese on Romaine Lettuce

4	fresh beets, peeled or 1 can of beets		4	large Romaine lettuce leaves
	Olive oil		4	tablespoons goat cheese
2	tablespoons butter		4	hard-boiled eggs
1	medium red onion, sliced		1	Fuji apple, cut into eighths
	Lawry's lemon pepper (to taste)			Red Wine and Mustard Vinaigrette Dressing (see page 71)
	Salt (to taste)			

> Preheat the oven to 375 degrees.

> Rub the beets with olive oil. Bake for around 25 minutes, or until soft. (You can cook them in the microwave in a bowl with a little water for around 20 minutes.) When cool, slice the beets.

> In a skillet, melt the butter over medium heat. Add the onion and sauté for 5 to 7 minutes, or until soft.

> Add the beets and season with the lemon pepper and salt.

> Divide the lettuce between two salad plates.

> Divide the onion mixture between the salads, spreading it evenly over the lettuce.

> Sprinkle 2 tablespoons of goat cheese over each salad.

> Arrange a hard-boiled egg on both sides of each plate.

> Arrange 2 apples slices on either side of each plate.

> Serve with the Red Wine and Mustard Vinaigrette Dressing.

Yield: 2 salads

Any one of the breads in this book, sliced, buttered, and grilled would go great with this salad!

Asparagus with Goat Cheese and Ginger Dressing over Spinach

12	spears white asparagus
12	spears green asparagus
4	hard-boiled eggs
4	cups fresh spinach, washed
2	cups crumbled goat cheese

	Ginger Sauce (see page 61)
1/2	cup Ginger Pieces (see page 61)
1/4	cup fresh berries
2	slices Basic Whole Wheat Bread (see page 34)

> Steam the white and green asparagus over medium heat for about 10 minutes, or until cooked to taste.

> Peel the hard-boiled eggs and slice each egg into 4 wedges.

> Divide the fresh spinach leaves between two large plates.

> Divide the asparagus between the plates. With the tips of the asparagus facing the outside of the plate, arrange them in bunches, alternating three green, three white, three green, three white.

> Between each bunch of asparagus, place two wedges of hard boiled egg lying flat, tip to tip.

> Mound 1 cup of goat cheese in the middle of each salad.

> Over the goat cheese, drizzle a little bit of the Ginger Sauce and then sprinkle 1/4 cup of the ginger pieces over each salad. Scatter 2 tablespoons berries over each salad.

> Serve each salad with a side of Ginger Sauce and a slice of buttered and grilled Basic Whole Wheat Bread.

Yield: 2 salads

CHAPTER SEVEN

Soups

Just a little creative spark turns anything into soup! Since soups and salads are great complements to sandwiches, I couldn't write this book without giving you at least a few.

Soups and salads stand together or individually as great meals with just a slice of grilled bread on the side. That's something to consider when you're in the mood for a light meal.

Nearly all my soups are vegan. (Adding sour cream or yogurt on top, which I like to do, negates that claim, of course.) Add whatever you like to the soups: nuts, fresh herbs, cheese, anything you find to further the already grand flavor and nutritional value. Use your imagination!

Cream of Broccoli Soup

Although I use soy milk, I called this "cream" because it is as good as any creamed soup. And besides "Soy Milk of Broccoli Soup" just doesn't have a good ring to it.

3	pounds broccoli florets and stems		1	teaspoon sweet dried basil
1	to 2 cups soy milk		1	teaspoon dill weed
1	tablespoon Lawry's lemon pepper			Cheddar cheese (to taste)
1	teaspoon salt			

> Put the broccoli in a soup pot and cover with water two inches above the broccoli.

> Bring to a full boil and cook until the broccoli is tender and you can easily poke a fork into it. *Be careful not to burn or overcook broccoli. It severely alters the taste.*

> Drain the water into a bowl and reserve it. Place the broccoli in a bowl.

> Put enough cooked broccoli into a food processor to reach halfway up the side. Add just enough reserved water to make blending easy. Be careful not to burn yourself.

> Process until smooth, then return to the soup pot.

> Repeat this procedure until all the broccoli is puréed. *Keep the soup on the thicker side, because you'll be adding soy milk.*

> Add the soy milk, lemon pepper, salt, basil, and dill weed, and mix.

> Serve hot with some cheese and a few mixed nuts on top.

Yield: 6 to 8 servings

For a light meal, serve this soup with a slice of grilled Spicy White Pepper-Jack Bread (see page 19) or Horseradish Parmesan (see page 4) and any of the salads (see pages 163 to 179).

Apple-Eggplant Soup

One morning as I prepared to make apple bran muffins, I eyed a zucchini and eggplant at the end of the counter. They were scheduled for a veggie sandwich later that day. They never made it. Apple-eggplant soup? Bulls-eye!

4	apples, peeled, cored, and chopped
2	large eggplants, peeled and chopped
2	to 3 cups vanilla soy milk
2	tablespoons packed brown sugar
2	tablespoons fresh lemon juice
1	tablespoon grated lemon zest
1	tablespoon Lawry's lemon pepper
1	to 2 teaspoons salt
1/2	teaspoon allspice
	Apple slices

> Put the apples and eggplant in a soup pot and add water to cover by two inches. (Reserve a few apple slices for garnish.)

> Bring to a full boil. Cook until the apples and eggplant are tender and you can easily poke a fork into them.

> Drain the water into a bowl and reserve it. Place the apples and eggplant into a bowl.

> Put enough apples and eggplant into a food processor to reach halfway up the side. Add the reserved water to reach one to two inches from the top. Be careful not to fill it too full or it will explode. (Wear long oven mitts when blending just in case it's a little too full. You don't want to burn yourself.)

> Pour the puréed mixture back into the pot. Repeat this procedure until all the apples and eggplant are puréed. Keep the soup on the thicker side because you'll be adding soy milk.

> Add the soy milk, brown sugar, lemon juice, lemon zest, lemon pepper, salt, and allspice, and mix.

> Serve hot with a mint sprig and apple slice on top.

Yield: 4 to 6 servings

For a light meal, consider a slice of grilled Brown Harvest Bread (see page 46) and any of the salads (see pages 163 to 179).

Celery Soup

This soup is delicious and contains great dietary fiber. I keep the stringy celery fibers in because I like them, and they're part of the fiber. To eliminate them, just strain the soup.

2	celery bunches, chopped (use the leafy greens)
1	to 2 cups soy milk
1	cup fresh, finely diced basil
1	tablespoon Lawry's lemon pepper
1	to 2 teaspoons salt
1	teaspoon dill weed
	Cheese and parsley for garnish

> Put the celery in a soup pot and cover with water two inches above the celery.

> Bring it to a full boil and cook until the celery is tender and you can easily poke a fork into it.

> Drain the water into a bowl and reserve it. Place the celery in a bowl.

> Put enough cooked celery into a food processor to reach halfway up the side. Add a small portion of the reserved water—just enough to make blending easy. Blend until smooth. Be careful not to burn yourself.

> Pour the blended mixture back into the soup pot.

> Repeat this procedure until all the celery is blended. *Keep the soup on the thicker side, because you'll be adding soy milk.*

> Add the soy milk, basil, lemon pepper, salt, and dill weed and mix.

> Serve hot and garnish with a dollop of cheese and parsley sprig.

Yield: 4 to 6 servings

For a light meal, serve this soup with a slice of grilled Spicy White Pepper-Jack Bread (see page 19) or Roasted Red Pepper Brie Mint Bread (see page 12) and any of the salads (see pages 163 to 179).

Honey Carrot Soup

Talk about rich in Vitamin A and beta-carotene! This soup is also versatile. On cold wintry days, this hot soup will keep you toasty and comfortable. On summer days, it can be served cool as a respite from the intense heat that can be served up by the season.

2	pounds carrots, peeled and chopped		1	tablespoon Lawry's lemon pepper
1	to 2 cups vanilla soy milk		1	teaspoon salt
½	cup honey (or to taste)		1	teaspoon dill weed
½	cup finely diced fresh basil			

> Put the carrots in a soup pot, and cover with water two inches above the carrots.

> Bring to a full boil and cook until the carrots are soft and tender and you can easily poke a fork into them.

> Drain the water into a bowl and reserve it. Place the carrots in a bowl.

> Fill a food processor half full of cooked carrots. Add just enough reserved water to make blending easy. Be careful not to burn yourself.

> Process until smooth, then pour the purée back into the soup pot.

> Repeat this procedure until all the carrots are puréed. *Keep the soup on the thick side, because you'll be adding soy milk.*

> Add the soy milk, honey, basil, lemon pepper, salt, and dill weed, and mix.

> Serve hot with a mint sprig and dollop of vanilla yogurt.

Yield: 6 servings

For a light meal, serve with a slice of grilled Horseradish Parmesan Bread (see page 4) or Honey-Nut Whole Wheat Bread (see page 41) and any of the salads (see pages 163 to 179).

Autumn Squash Soup

Growing up in the bitter, windy winters of Chicago were oftentimes brutal. It wasn't an odd thing at all to walk home from school, about six blocks, and be blue from head to toe. Regardless of how many layers you wore, the bite of winter always seemed to get to the bone. One of the quickest ways to warm up was to remove your boots and throw your feet onto the steaming radiator until Mom hollered "Soup's ready!" Ahhhh, hot soup!

1	acorn squash	2	cups roasted, sliced almonds (see page 203)
1	spaghetti squash	1/4	cup finely chopped fresh basil leaves
1	summer squash	2	tablespoons Lawry's lemon pepper
4	to 6 cups warm water	2	tablespoons dill weed
2	cups vanilla soy milk (more for thinner soup, less for thicker soup)	1	teaspoon salt
2	cups vanilla yogurt	1/2	cup honey (add more or less depending on your sweet tooth)
1	cup finely diced red onion	1	to 1 1/4 cups goat cheese
2	celery stalks, finely chopped		

> Microwave the squashes until they are soft, about 15 minutes on high. Let them cool. Cut them into halves, scoop out the seeds, and transfer the meat to a blender. You will probably need to blend the squash in 4 to 6 batches.

> Add about 1/4 to 1/2 cup warm water to the blender, just enough to liquefy the squash but keep it thick. Be careful not to burn yourself. Purée the squash in the blender, and then transfer it to a large saucepan. Continue until all the squash is puréed.

> Add the soy milk, yogurt, onion, celery, almonds, basil, lemon pepper, dill weed, salt, and honey, and bring to a boil over a high heat. Reduce the heat to low and simmer for about 20 minutes.

> Add a dollop of goat cheese on top before serving.

Yield: 8 to 10 servings

For a complete meal, serve this soup with a grilled slice of Horseradish Parmesan Bread (see page 4) and a salad of your choice.

Black Bean and Barley Soup

Beans are a great source of iron, as is barley. This is a hearty soup best suited for winter. However, if you keep this soup on the thick side—I mean really thick—you can use these beans as an addition to tacos or burritos or use as a side dish for any meal.

3	cups dried black beans
10	cups water
1	cup Scotch barley (uncooked)
1	cup finely diced red onions
1	cup sliced mushrooms
2	tablespoons Lawry's lemon pepper

2	teaspoons salt
1/8	teaspoon cayenne pepper (optional)
	Soy milk or water (as needed for thinning)
	Sour cream
	Maple Merlot Bread (see page 28)

> Put the black beans in a large saucepan and cover them with water. Soak them overnight, if possible, or at least for a few hours.

> When ready, drain the beans and pick out any bad or questionable beans. Put the good beans back in the soup pan and add 10 cups of water.

> Bring the beans to a roiling boil over high heat. Reduce the heat to low and simmer for 20 to 25 minutes, or until the water is boiled off. Reserve 1 cup of beans. Transfer the remaining beans to a blender. Be careful not to burn yourself. Purée the beans and then transfer them to a saucepan over low heat.

> Add the barley, onion, mushrooms, lemon pepper, salt, and cayenne pepper, if using. Mix well, cover, and simmer for at least 1 hour, stirring occasionally. If it needs thinning, add a little soy milk or water.

> Serve hot with a dollop of sour cream on top of each bowl and a slice of Maple Merlot Bread and a salad.

Yield: 8 to 10 servings

Potato Soup

My mother made the first homemade potato soup I tasted. It was so thick and creamy. She added sour cream and ched-dar cheese to it. It was out of this world! This is my version of my mother's soup. I've added lots of vegetables, but you can add more or omit some, as you please.

10	potatoes, peeled and chopped		2	tablespoons Lawry's lemon pepper
	Water or milk (as needed to thin soup)		1	tablespoon salt
2	cups fresh, leafy spinach		1	tablespoon dill weed
2	cups sliced button mushrooms		2	teaspoons celery salt
2	cups finely chopped celery stalks		2	cups sour cream
2	cups chopped broccoli florets		2	cups shredded Cheddar cheese
1	cup finely diced fresh basil leaves			Spicy White Pepper-Jack Bread (see page 19)

> In a large saucepan combine the potatoes and water to cover. Bring to a boil over high heat.

> Reduce the heat to medium low and continue boiling the potatoes until they're soft and you can easily stick a fork through them.

> When done, remove the potatoes from the heat and drain the water into a large bowl.

> Put the potatoes into a blender. Add some of the reserved potato water and purée. (You will probably have to purée the potatoes in batches.) To avoid burning yourself, use long oven mitts or a folded towel to hold the top of the blender. Pour the puréed potatoes back into the saucepan and turn the heat to medium high.

> Add water or milk until the soup is your desired consistency.

> Add the spinach, mushrooms, celery, broccoli, basil, lemon pepper, salt, dill weed, and celery salt and mix well.

> Reduce the heat to low and simmer the soup for at least 45 minutes. The soup might thicken as it simmers. If it does, simply add a little more water or soy milk to keep it at the desired consistency.

> Top each bowl of soup with a dollop of sour cream and about 2 tablespoons cheddar cheese.

> Serve hot with a grilled slice of Spicy White Pepper-Jack Bread and a salad.

Yield: 10 to 12 servings

Pumpkin Soup

Pumpkins are mostly considered a holiday fruit, but I eat pumpkin all year long. It makes a great hot soup for the autumn and winter. Since it makes a magnificent cold soup, too, it is also great in the summer. It's extremely high in vitamin A and beta-carotene.

4	(16-ounce) cans Libby's 100% pure pumpkin	4	teaspoons cinnamon, plus extra for garnish
6	cups milk, cream, or vanilla soy milk	1 ½	teaspoons salt
2	cups water	2	teaspoons ground cloves
4	to 5 cups maple syrup	2	teaspoons ground nutmeg
		2	cups vanilla yogurt

> In a large soup pot over medium heat, combine the pumpkin, milk, water, maple syrup, cinnamon, salt, cloves, and nutmeg and mix very well with a wire whisk.

> Simmer for 15 to 20 minutes and serve hot.

> Serve with a dollop of vanilla yogurt and a sprinkle of cinnamon.

Yield: 12 to 14 servings

For a complete meal, serve with a slice of French Bread (see page 27) and a salad of your choice. This is such a delicious meal!

Lentil Soup

Lentil soup is so easy to make, is highly nutritious and flavorful, and is a wonderful dietary fiber for the digestive system. You can't go wrong with this soup no matter what the season.

4	cups lentils, washed and sorted		2	teaspoons salt (or to taste)
10	cups water		2	cups shredded Cheddar cheese
	Water or soy milk (as needed to thin soup)		1	cup toasted, sliced almonds Honey-Nut Whole Wheat Bread (see page 41)
2	tablespoons Lawry's lemon pepper (or to taste)			

> Put the lentils and 10 cups of water in a large saucepan and bring to a boil over a high heat.

> Reduce the heat to low, cover the pan, and simmer until the water is all gone and the lentils are very soft.

> To thin the soup, add water or soy milk to obtain desired thickness.

> Add the lemon pepper and salt.

> Top with each bowl of soup with about 1/4 cup cheese and 2 tablespoons almonds and serve with a slice of grilled and buttered Honey-Nut Whole Wheat Bread and a salad.

Yield: 8 to 10 servings

Spinach Soup

Spinach is a great source of vitamin A and has a flavor all its own. Although frozen spinach doesn't have the flavor or nutritional value that fresh spinach has, it is better to eat it frozen than not at all. So use whichever you prefer for this soup.

4	(10-ounce) bags fresh, leafy spinach
2	tablespoons Lawry's lemon pepper
2	teaspoons salt
1	teaspoon sweet dried basil
	Water or soy milk (as needed to thin soup)
1/4	cup sour cream

> Set aside four cups of the spinach. Put the remaining spinach in a large soup pot and cover with water.

> Bring to a boil over high heat, then reduce the heat to low and simmer for about 8 minutes, or until the spinach is soft. Drain the water into a bowl.

> Put the spinach into a blender. Add just enough of the water to make the spinach easy to blend. Be careful not to burn yourself. Use oven mitts or a towel to hold the top of the blender as you purée the spinach.

> Put the puréed spinach back into the soup pot.

> Turn the heat to medium-low and add the lemon pepper, salt, basil, and enough of the water or soy milk to make it obtain desired consistency. Mix well.

> Let the soup simmer for 30 minutes for peak flavor.

> Serve with a dollop of sour cream on top of each bowl.

Yield: 4 to 6 servings

For a complete meal, serve the soup with a slice of grilled Brown Harvest Bread (see page 46) and a salad of your choice. This is a great combination lunch or dinner!

CHAPTER EIGHT

Sides and Accompaniments

According to ancient texts and saudiaramcoworld.com, as far back as 1700 bc the culinary arts, along with reading and writing, were considered professional rather than general skills . . . even down to the side dishes. Lentils, leeks, and shallots, as well as garlic and chickpeas, offered some savory sidesteps. In the ancient times grasshoppers were considered an additional delicacy to any meal. I'm not serving up any jiminy crickets here, but these dishes do complement any menu. I know you'll enjoy these simple feasts which are delicious as snacks as well as side dishes.

Cheddar Cheese Potatoes

1/2	cup (1 stick) butter	1	cup shredded Cheddar cheese
2	large potatoes, cut into rounds		Salt (to taste)

> Heat the oven to 375 degrees. Put the butter on a baking sheet, and place it in the oven to melt. It takes only a couple minutes, so don't let it burn!

> Remove the baking sheet from the oven and place the potato rounds on the sheet. Then turn them over so that each side is buttered.

Sprinkle with salt. Bake for about 20 minutes.

> With a spatula, gather the potatoes together so that they touch. Sprinkle the Cheddar cheese over them, and return them to the oven for a few minutes, until the cheese melts. Serve hot.

Yield: 2 servings

These potatoes make a superb snack or addition to any meal.

French String Beans & Roasted Almonds

1/4	cup (1/2 stick) butter	2	tablespoons fresh lemon zest
4	cups chopped, cleaned French string beans		Lemon pepper (to taste)
			Salt (to taste)
2	tablespoons fresh lemon juice		
2	cups sliced roasted almonds (see page 203)		

> In a large skillet, melt the butter over medium-low heat. Add the green beans, lemon juice, almonds, lemon zest, lemon pepper, and salt.

> Cover and cook for 5 minutes. If the beans are not tender enough for you, lower heat and cook for another 5 minutes, or until cooked to your taste.

Yield: 4 servings

Roasted Nuts

This recipe applies to all kinds of nuts. If you want dry roasted nuts, omit the oils and salts and simply roast to desired crispness and color.

Nuts   Salt (optional)
Oil

> Heat the oven to 400 degrees. Place the nuts on a baking sheet and drizzle them with olive oil. Put some oil in your hands, and mix the nuts around to coat them. Sprinkle them with salt, if desired.

> Cook for 10 to 15 minutes or to desired crispness and color. Let cool.

> Store in an airtight, dry container. They may be refrigerated or frozen.

Candied Walnuts

2	tablespoons butter		1/8	teaspoon salt
1/2	cup packed brown sugar		3	cups walnuts, whole or chopped
2	tablespoons honey			

> In a skillet, melt the butter. Add the brown sugar, honey, and salt. Mix until creamy. Add the walnuts and mix until they're coated. Remove them from the skillet and place on a plate or platter to cool.

Yield: 3 cups

Candied walnuts go well on salads, over ice cream, or just as a snack in a candy or nut bowl.

Herb Grain Breading

1 cup Bob's Red Mill 4- or 5-grain cereal mix

1/2 cup whole wheat flour

1 tablespoon sweet dried basil

1 tablespoon Lawry's lemon pepper

1 teaspoon dill weed

1 teaspoon diced fresh thyme

1 teaspoon dried tarragon

1 teaspoon salt

1/2 teaspoon dried oregano

Dash of allspice

> Mix together all the ingredients.

> To use as breading, dust meats or vegetables, with wheat flour, then dip and coat them in beaten eggs, and finally, fully coat with the Herb Grain Breading.

> Gently fry in butter, olive oil, or the oil of your choice.

Yield: 1 1/2 cups

Croutons

4 cups diced, crusty bread

1/4 cup olive oil

Lemon pepper (to taste)

Salt (to taste)

Garlic salt (to taste)

3 tablespoons finely chopped garlic

> Preheat the oven to 400 degrees.

> In a large mixing bowl, combine the bread, oil, lemon pepper, salt, garlic salt, and garlic and mix well until the bread is well coated. Add more olive oil if needed.

> Spread the coated bread on a baking sheet and bake for about 10 minutes, or until the bread is crispy.

> When cooled, store in an airtight container. Use on soups, in salads, or for snacking.

Yield: 4 cups

Using an assortment of different breads—especially leftovers from breads in this book—make the best croutons because there is a variety of flavors from the different breads.

Roasted Red Peppers

This technique works for most any vegetable. Watch the clock, because some veggies, such as broccoli, roast more quickly than others.

Red bell peppers
Olive oil

> Heat the oven to 400 degrees. Wash and dry the peppers well, rub them with olive oil, place on a baking sheet, and bake for 20 to 30 minutes. When done, they'll be soft.

> Under cold running water, peel off the outer layer and discard the seeds inside. Let cool.

> Store in an airtight, dry container. They may be refrigerated or frozen.

Broccoli, Cheddar Cheese, and Pine Nuts

This is one of those side dishes that's fantastic with an entrée or as a snack on its own. It's one of my favorites as a solo snack because it's easy to prepare and is very tasty and nutritious.

2	crowns broccoli		Salt (to taste)
2	tablespoons water (optional)	2	cups shredded Cheddar cheese
2	tablespoons butter	1	cup pine nuts
	Lemon pepper (to taste)		

> Clean the broccoli and put in a large microwaveable bowl. Add the water, if desired, and cook in the microwave for 5 to 6 minutes, or until tender.

> If you've used water, drain it from the bowl, add the butter, lemon pepper, salt, cheese, and nuts to the bowl and mix everything very well.

> If the cheese needs to be melted more, pop the bowl back into the microwave for 30 seconds.

Yield: 2 servings

I know a woman who insists she never uses the microwave. She says it's bad for you, yet, every time she's at my home, she's popping things in and out of the microwave. Now, I rarely use the microwave, but I think it is a wonderful invention. Well, one day I confronted her on her microwave use, and she looked me straight away in the eyes and said, with perfect seriousness, "I only ever use it at your house."

Spinach, Mushrooms, Swiss Cheese, and Roasted Almonds

Quite often when I make this as a side dish with an entrée, I omit the cheese because I know Swiss cheese demands a particular audience. When I make it as a snack for myself, I never leave out the Swiss cheese. Of course, you're free to use any cheese you like. I just happen to think the combinations of flavors are so well suited.

2	tablespoons butter
4	cups sliced fresh mushrooms
2	cups roasted almonds (see page 203)
10	(12-ounce) bags cleaned fresh, spinach

	Lemon pepper (to taste)
	Salt (to taste)
2	cups shredded Swiss cheese

> In a skillet, melt the butter over medium heat and add the mushrooms. Sauté for about 10 minutes, or until they're a crispy brown.

> Add the almonds and sauté until heated through, about 5 minutes.

> Add the spinach and sauté until cooked, about 7 minutes. Drain the water.

> Add the lemon pepper and salt and mix well.

> Add the cheese, cover the skillet with a lid, and reduce the heat to low. Cook for 1 to 2 more minutes.

> Serve hot.

Yield: 2 to 4 servings

Acorn Squash with Brown Sugar and Butter

1	acorn squash
4	tablespoons packed brown sugar
4	tablespoons butter
	Salt (to taste)

> Make 2 to 4 deep slits into the sides of the acorn squash and microwave it for 15 to 20 minutes, depending on the size. When you can easily stick a knife or fork through the middle and the ends, it's done.

> Remove the squash and let it cool for a few minutes. Wearing oven mitts slice the squash into halves lengthwise. Spoon out the seeds and discard them.

> Divide the butter and brown sugar evenly between the squashes. Stir the butter and brown sugar into the meat of the squashes, using the skin as a bowl. Season the squashes with a little salt to bring out the flavor and serve.

Yield: 2 servings

Long Grain Wild Rice with Whole Mushrooms, Goat Cheese, and Sun-Dried Tomatoes

1	(6-ounce) box Uncle Ben's Long Grain Wild Rice
4	tablespoons butter
2	cups white button mushrooms
2	cups chopped sun-dried tomatoes
8	tablespoons goat cheese (optional)
3	tablespoons sour cream
1	sprig parsley

> Prepare the rice according to the package.

> In a skillet, melt the butter over medium-low heat. Add the mushrooms and sun-dried tomatoes and cook until tender, about 10 minutes.

> In a mixing bowl, combine the cooked rice, mushrooms, and tomatoes. Sprinkle the cheese over the rice dish.

> Garnish the center with the sour cream and parsley.

> Serve hot or cold.

Yield: 3 to 4 servings

Baby Snap Peas with Garlic, Mint, and Croutons

2	tablespoons butter
1/2	cup minced garlic
1/2	cup finely chopped fresh mint leaves
1	cup croutons (preferably homemade, see page 204)
4	cups baby snap peas
	Lemon pepper (to taste)
	Salt (to taste)

> In a skillet, melt the butter over medium-low heat. Add the garlic and mint leaves and sauté, stirring frequently, for about 8 minutes, or until the garlic is browned.

> Add the croutons and cook until thoroughly heated.

> Add the baby snap peas, lemon pepper, and salt. Mix everything very well.

Yield: 4 servings

You only want to warm the baby snap peas while they're in the skillet because they are best crispy and sweet.

CHAPTER NINE

Bountiful Breakfasts

With my busy schedule, sitting down to an enjoyable breakfast is a Saturday or Sunday luxury. Often, I'll invite friends and throw a morning party: superb coffee, relaxing mimosas, mouthwatering pastries, and perhaps a substantial (and delicious!) egg/tofu scramble. Here are a few recipes I know you'll enjoy.

Basic Egg or Tofu Scramble

6	slices turkey bacon
2	plus 2 plus 2 tablespoons butter
2	slices Basic Whole Wheat Bread (see page 34)
1	cup diced red onions
2	cups chopped tomatoes
4	cups fresh spinach

6	eggs, beaten, or 14 ounces firm crumbled tofu (or half of each)
	Lawry's lemon pepper (to taste)
	Salt (to taste)
1	cup shredded Cheddar cheese Cheddar Cheese Potatoes (see page 200)

> In a skillet or on a griddle, cook the turkey bacon strips to desired crispness.

> Toast the bread slices and spread 2 tablespoons of the butter over them.

> In another skillet, melt 2 tablespoons of the butter over low to medium heat.

> Add the red onions and cook until caramelized (a translucent tan).

> Add the tomatoes and spinach and cook until the spinach is wilted.

> Add the eggs or tofu and stir until the eggs are scrambled or the tofu is hot.

> Add the lemon pepper and salt and mix well.

> Sprinkle the Cheddar cheese over the mixture and cover. Keep over low heat until the cheese is melted.

> Divide the egg or tofu mixture evenly between two plates. Divide the turkey bacon between the two plates.

> Spread the remaining butter on the toast.

> Serve with Cheddar Cheese Potatoes.

Yield: 2 servings

Many people like eggs and tofu together. It's great protein and flavor!

French Toast

For tasty French toast, soak the bread in the batter for at least an hour before grilling. Overnight is even better. But for the best possible fare, slice the loaf of bread fresh from the oven, let cool just slightly, then dunk into the batter.

6   eggs
1   cup packed brown sugar
1   cup half-and-half
4   thick slices French Bread
     (see page 27)
     Butter

     Powdered sugar
     Raspberries and blackberries
     for garnish
     Butter, softened
     Maple syrup, warmed
1   Fruit Cup (see page 246)

> In a large bowl, combine the eggs, brown sugar, and half-and-half.

> Cut the slices of bread in half. Soak them in the egg batter until they're completely saturated.

> In a skillet or on a griddle, cook them over medium-low heat until brown. Flip them to brown the other side.

> When they're hot all the way through, put them on a plate, smother with oodles of butter, and coat with powdered sugar.

> Sprinkle powdered sugar lightly all over the plate, then garnish with fresh raspberries and blackberries. Serve with a side of fresh, soft butter, warm maple syrup, and a fresh Fruit Cup.

Yield: 4 servings

Ginger Egg or Tofu Scramble

This is my personal favorite!

6	slices turkey bacon
2	tablespoons plus 2 tablespoons plus 2 tablespoons butter
2	slices Brown Harvest Bread (see page 46)
2	tablespoons Ginger Sauce (see page 61)
1	cup broccoli florets
2	cups fresh spinach

1/4	cup Ginger Pieces (see page 61)
1/2	cup Roasted Almonds (see page 203)
6	eggs, beaten, or 14 ounces crumbled firm tofu (or half of each)
1/2	cup crumbled goat cheese
	Lawry's lemon pepper (to taste)
	Salt (to taste)
	Cheddar Cheese Potatoes (see page 200)

> In a skillet or on a griddle, cook the turkey bacon to desired crispness.

> Spread 2 tablespoons of butter on the bread slices and grill them, or if you prefer, toast and then butter them.

> In another skillet, melt 2 tablespoons of the butter over medium-low heat.

> Add the Ginger Sauce. Add the broccoli and cook until tender. Add the spinach, Ginger Pieces, and Roasted Almonds, and mix. Add the eggs or tofu, and cook, stirring until the eggs are scrambled or the tofu is hot. Add the lemon pepper and salt and mix well.

> Sprinkle the goat cheese over the mixture, turn off the heat, and cover until the goat cheese melts.

> Divide the egg or tofu mixture evenly between two plates. Divide the turkey bacon between the two.

> Spread the remaining butter on the Brown Harvest toast.

> Serve with Cheddar Cheese Potatoes.

Yield: 2 servings

Pesto Egg or Tofu Scramble

6	slices turkey bacon
2	tablespoons plus 2 tablespoons plus 2 tablespoons butter
2	English Muffins (see page 24)
1	cup diced red onions
2	cups sliced mushrooms
1	cup broccoli florets
4	cups chopped fresh spinach

6	eggs, beaten, or 14 ounces firm crumbled tofu (or half of each)
	Lawry's lemon pepper (to taste)
	Salt (to taste)
1	cup Pesto Sauce (see page 66)
1	cup shredded Monterey Jack cheese
	Cheddar Cheese Potatoes (see page 200)

> In a skillet or on a griddle, cook the turkey bacon to desired crispness.

> Spread 2 tablespoons of the butter over the English Muffins and grill them, or if you prefer, toast and then butter them.

> In another skillet, melt 2 tablespoons of the butter over medium-low heat.

> Add the onions and mushrooms and cook until the onions are caramelized (a translucent tan) and the mushrooms are dark brown.

> Add the broccoli and spinach. Reduce the heat and cover, cooking until the broccoli is tender.

> Add the eggs or tofu and cook, stirring until the eggs are scrambled or the tofu is hot.

> Season with lemon pepper and salt and mix.

> Add the Pesto Sauce and mix.

> Sprinkle the cheese over the mixture and cover. Keep over very low heat until the cheese is melted.

> Divide the egg or tofu mixture evenly between two plates. Divide the turkey bacon between the two.

> Spread the remaining butter on the English Muffins.

> Serve with Cheddar Cheese Potatoes.

Yield: 2 servings

Granola

1	(16-ounce) package Bob's Red Mill 5-grain cereal mix
1	(25-ounce) package Bob's Red Mill 10-grain cereal mix
2	cups rolled oats
2	cups sliced almonds
1	cup packed brown sugar
3/4	cups honey
2	cups vanilla soy milk

> Preheat the oven to 400 degrees. On a baking sheet, with your hands (so that you know the ingredients are thoroughly mixed), combine the 5- and 10-grain cereal mixes, rolled oats, almonds, brown sugar, honey, and soy milk.

> Bake for 20 to 25 minutes. Stir the granola frequently while it bakes to ensure complete baking.

Yield: 8 to 10 servings

Chopped apples and raisins are excellent with this granola mix.
Add as many as you like. Raisins burn quickly, though, so mix them around often while in the oven.

10-Grain Pancakes

These pancakes are out of this world! Not only are they the healthiest pancakes you'll ever eat, but nothing compares with their taste.

1	cup Bob Mill's 10-grain cereal mix
1/2	cup Bob Mill's 5-grain cereal mix
1/2	cup whole bran flakes (not the cereal, but the bran kernel)
4	heaping tablespoons brown sugar
1	teaspoon baking powder
1/2	teaspoon baking soda
1/4	teaspoon salt

2	eggs
1	teaspoon pure vanilla extract
1	teaspoon pure almond extract
1	cup vanilla soy milk
4	tablespoons butter plus extra for serving Maple syrup
1	Fruit Cup (see page 246)

> In a large bowl, combine the cereal mixes, bran flakes, brown sugar, baking powder, baking soda, and salt.

> In a medium bowl, combine the eggs, vanilla extract, almond extract, and milk.

> Add the wet ingredients to the dry ingredients and mix.

> In a skillet or on a griddle, melt the butter over low to medium heat.

> Drop 3 heaping tablespoons of batter per pancake into the skillet.

> Cook until the batter bubbles all over the top of the pancake. Flip and bake until the pancake puffs up and becomes firm. Be careful not to burn them; they can burn quickly.

> Serve with lots of butter, warm maple syrup, and a fresh Fruit Cup.

Yield: 4 (1-pancake) servings

Turkey Breakfast Bun

This breakfast is served open faced. Though I consider it a breakfast, it is often requested as a lunch item, too. This is a healthy portion, and eating both halves is enough to fill you for the entire morning and a good deal of the afternoon. Since it's very good reheated, don't feel you must eat it all at once.

2	plus 1 tablespoons butter
1	pound sliced turkey
	Lawry's lemon pepper (to taste)
	Salt (to taste)
1	cup Tangy Apricot Pineapple Sauce (see page 82)
1/2	cup chopped tomatoes
1	cup shredded Monterey Jack cheese
1	English Muffin, sliced (see page 24)

> In a skillet, melt 2 tablespoons of the butter over medium-low heat.

> Add the turkey, lemon pepper, and salt and mix well to coat the turkey with the butter.

> Add the Tangy Apricot Pineapple Sauce and the tomatoes and mix well until the turkey is coated with the sauce.

> Sprinkle the shredded cheese evenly over the turkey mixture.

> Cover with a lid and turn off the heat.

> Spread the last tablespoon of butter evenly over the English Muffin halves and grill, or else toast the English Muffin halves and then butter.

> Place the English Muffin halves on a plate.

> Slide the turkey mixture over the English Muffins and serve with a side of Tangy Apricot Pineapple Sauce.

> Garnish with a few berries and grapes.

Yield: 1 serving

Sweet Muffins

Sweet Bread is a cinch to make and has a creamy, buttery flavor with just the right amount of sweetness. A wonderful pastry to have with morning coffee or for a mid-afternoon snack.

1	batch Sweet Dough (see page 17)
1/2	cup plus 4 tablespoons butter, melted
1	cup packed brown sugar

> Preheat the oven to 375 degrees. In a large bowl, combine 1/2 cup of the butter and the brown sugar and mix well.

> Add the Sweet Dough, and with your hands, mix everything together until thoroughly combined. Even then, it will look like lumps of dough.

> With the remaining butter, generously butter a 6-count muffin tin. Fill each compartment to the brim or just over. Let the dough rise for 45 to 60 minutes.

> Bake for 25 to 30 minutes.

> Remove the rolls from the muffin tin immediately and let them cool slightly, but serve warm.

Yield: 6 large pastries, 6 servings

The sweet breads get very large and, like the cinnamon rolls, will drip so place a baking sheet or foil underneath the tins to catch any overflow. For extra sweetness, drizzle a little cinnamon roll Icing over the top (see page 230).

Apple Bran Muffins

Here is a healthful and flavorful morning muffin. It's also great as a mid-morning or afternoon snack. In fact, it's great any time of day or night!

3	cups whole wheat flour
1	(16-ounce) package Bob's Red Mill 5-grain cereal mix
1	(17-ounce) box 100% bran cereal
1	tablespoon baking powder
1	teaspoon baking soda
1	teaspoon salt

3	cups vanilla soy milk
1	cup packed brown sugar
1/2	cup olive oil
3	tablespoons dark molasses
5	to 6 apples, peeled and chopped
2	cups raisins (optional)

> Preheat the oven to 375 degrees. In a large bowl, combine the flour, 5-grain mix, bran cereal, baking powder, baking soda, and salt.

> In another large bowl, combine the soy milk, brown sugar, olive oil, and molasses.

> Add the soy milk mixture to the flour mixture and mix well.

> Stir in the apples and raisins.

> Generously butter the muffin tin.

> Fill each compartment to the brim or just over.

> Bake for 25 to 30 minutes.

> Cool, but serve warm and drizzle with maple syrup or honey.

Yield: 8 to 10 large or 10 to 12 small muffins

This batter can be refrigerated for a couple days. The muffins are also delicious with cinnamon roll icing (see page 230) or drizzle a little honey or maple syrup over them.

Cinnamon Rolls

These cinnamon rolls are the best. They get huge and will drip, so place a baking sheet or foil underneath the tins to catch any overflow. They're terrific for breakfast with coffee or milk, but they're also a good snack or dessert.

Rolls

1	batch Sweet Dough (see page 17)
4	tablespoons all-purpose flour
1	cup (2 sticks) butter, melted
2	cups packed brown sugar
3	tablespoons cinnamon
4	tablespoons butter

Icing

4	cups powdered sugar
2	cups half-and-half (for a richer icing, use heavy whipping cream)

For the rolls:

> Preheat the oven to 375 degrees. Sprinkle the flour on the countertop or a very large cutting board. You'll need lots of room to roll out the Sweet Dough. Roll it so that the long side is perpendicular to your body. The dough should be only slightly thicker than paper thin.

> In a large bowl, combine the melted butter, brown sugar, and cinnamon and mix well.

> Spread the cinnamon mixture over the dough to the very edges.

> With your hands, tightly roll the dough into a loaf, with the rolling action going away from your body. To hold in the fillings, fold the outer edges of the dough as you roll.

> Cut into 6 to 8 cinnamon rolls.

> Grease the muffin tins with the remaining 4 tablespoons butter. Use more if necessary.

> Place the cut cinnamon rolls into the muffin tins. Let them rise for 45 to 60 minutes.

> Bake for 18 to 20 minutes, 15 for smaller rolls. Keep an eye on them.

> Use oven mitts to immediately remove the muffins from the tins.

For the icing:

> In a large bowl, mix the powdered sugar and half-and-half. For a thinner icing, use more half-and-half.

> Spread on the cooled cinnamon rolls.

Yield: 6 to 8 large rolls

This icing enhances any pastry or roll, and it's so simple to make!

Lemon Meringue Pie

This lemon filling is delicious, and so the recipe calls for more than average. If it's too much filling for you, cut the amount in half, but leave the Piecrust and Meringue recipes as they are for accurate proportions.

2	cups sugar
3/4	cup cornstarch
1	cup water
2	cups fresh lemon juice
6	egg yolks

6	tablespoons butter
1	cup lemon zest
	Prebaked 9-inch Piecrust (see page 234)
	Meringue (see page 234)

> In a saucepan, mix together the sugar and cornstarch. Gradually stir in the water and 2 cups of the lemon juice.

> Over low to medium heat, stirring constantly, cook the ingredients until they come to a boil. Boil, while stirring, for one minute. (If you stop stirring, the mixture will clump.)

> Remove the mixture from the heat and stir half of it into the egg yolks. Blend the egg yolk mixture back into the saucepan, mixing well to avoid clumping. Bring to a boil and boil for another minute, stirring constantly.

> Remove the mixture from the heat, add the butter and lemon zest and mix well with a wire whisk.

> Preheat the oven to 400 degrees.

> Pour into a prebaked 9-inch Piecrust. Cover with Meringue.

> Bake for 10 to 12 minutes or until the meringue is firm and the peaks are brown. Be careful not to burn the peaks.

> Cool before serving.

Yield: One 9-inch pie (6 to 8 servings)

Pumpkin Pie

I'm so proud of this velvety and creamy pumpkin pie. I've never tasted better.

1	(29-ounce) can Libby's 100% pure pumpkin
20	ounces (2 1/2 cups) vanilla soy milk
3/4	cup powdered sugar
3/4	cup packed brown sugar
3	tablespoons dark rum
1	shot espresso coffee
1	tablespoon cinnamon
3/4	teaspoon salt
3/4	teaspoon ginger
1/2	teaspoon ground cloves
1/4	teaspoon nutmeg
4	eggs, beaten
1	9-inch unbaked Piecrust (see page 234)

> Preheat the oven to 425 degrees. In a large bowl, combine pumpkin, soy milk, sugar, brown sugar, rum, coffee, cinnamon, salt, ginger, cloves, and nutmeg and mix well.

> Add the eggs to the pumpkin mixture and mix well.

> Pour the pumpkin mixture into an unbaked 9-inch pie shell. (The filling will go to the top. Personally, I prefer one large and abundant pie, but you can make this into two pies.)

> Bake for 20 minutes. Reduce the heat to 350 degrees, and bake another 50 to 60 minutes. To check for doneness, insert a knife in the middle of the pie. It should come out clean.

> Cool for 2 to 3 hours before serving. Store in the refrigerator.

Yield: One 9-inch pie (6 to 8 servings)

Two-Ton Bittersweet Chocolate Fudge Cake

All cocoa powders have different consistencies, which alters the consistency of the cakes. In order to keep the cake moist, you may need to use more or less (probably less) if you're not able to find Ambrosia's chocolate. Experimenting is and always will be half the fun in baking! This cake is very dense and VERY moist. It is NOT a light, fluffy cake. It's fabulously rich, heavy, and decadent!

2	cups (4 sticks or 1 pound) butter
10	ounces unsweetened chocolate
6	eggs
2	cups sugar
1/2	cup maple syrup
2	cups all-purpose flour

> Preheat the oven to 350 degrees. In a saucepan over low heat, melt the butter and chocolate, mixing well. Let it boil on low heat for 2 minutes.

Remove the chocolate mixture from the stove and pour it into a large mixing bowl. Add the eggs, sugar, and maple syrup. Mix together very well.

> Add the flour and mix well.

> Generously butter three 9-inch cake pans and dust with flour.

> Divide the batter evenly among the cake pans. Use a measuring cup for accuracy.

> Bake for 15 to 18 minutes, checking often.

> Cool and frost with Bittersweet Chocolate Frosting (see page 235).

Yield: One 3-layer cake

Ovens vary. Test your cake by inserting a toothpick that should come out clean.

The Best Carrot Cake

2	cups all-purpose flour
2	teaspoons baking powder
2	teaspoons baking soda
2	teaspoons cinnamon
1/8	teaspoon nutmeg
1/8	teaspoon cloves
1	cup whole, salted, Roasted Almonds (see page 203)
1	cup Roasted Pine Nuts (see page 203)
1	cup olive oil
1	cup sugar
1/2	cup (1 stick) butter, melted
1/2	cup packed brown sugar

4	eggs
3	tablespoons dark molasses
2	tablespoons maple syrup
2	cups chopped fresh pineapple, or 1 (16-ounce) can crushed pineapple, drained
3	heaping cups shredded carrots

Frosting

4	(8-ounce) packages cream cheese (room temperature)
2	sticks (1 cup) butter (room temperature)
2	cups powdered sugar
	Half-and-half (as needed)

> Preheat the oven to 350 degrees. In a large bowl, combine the flour, baking powder, baking soda, cinnamon, nutmeg, cloves, almonds, and pine nuts and mix very well.

> In another large bowl, combine the olive oil, sugar, butter, brown sugar, eggs, molasses, maple syrup, pineapple, and carrots and mix well. Add them to the dry mixture. Mix *very* well.

> Generously butter three 9-inch cake pans and dust with flour. Divide the cake batter evenly into the cake pans. Use a measuring cup for accuracy.

> Bake for 20 to 25 minutes.

> Insert a toothpick into the cakes to make sure they are done. The toothpick should come out clean. Cool in pans for 10 minutes. Remove and cool completely.

To make the frosting:

> With an electric mixer, mix the cream cheese, butter, sugar, and powdered sugar until fluffy, but stiff. Add half-and-half to thin.

> Use the frosting to fill and frost the cooled layers.

Yield: One 3-layer cake

Fruit Cup

This is a healthful addition to French Toast (see page 219) or 10-Grain Pancakes (see page 225).
In addition to serving as a good side dish to any meal, it's also a yummy snack.

1	tablespoon fresh raspberries
1	tablespoon fresh blackberries
1	tablespoon fresh blueberries
1/4	banana, sliced in rounds
2	slices kiwi
3	thin apple wedges
1	tablespoon Plum Jam Sauce (see page 69)

> In a small bowl, combine the raspberries, blackberries, blueberries, and banana.

> On one side of the bowl, garnish with the kiwi, and on the other side of the bowl, garnish with the apples. Drizzle the Plum Jam Sauce over all.

Yield: 1 serving

T H A N K S !

I'd like to thank you for buying this book, considering that an unbelievable number of cook-books line the shelves of bookstores and grocery stores. I hope you experience some of the pleasure that baking, cooking, and creating recipes have brought me, my family, and guests.

If you're a newcomer to the wonderful world of baking and cooking, I hope I've made the book as understandable as possible. I took extra time on the instructions which, in some cases, might seem unusually long, but I wanted you to be able to follow them easily.

If you're a pro in the kitchen, I hope these recipes keep you involved and interested. Mostly, I hope you taste the delightfully blended flavors in my combinations of foods.

God bless and peace,
Margaux Sky

P.S. If you haven't time for ambitious baking or sauce making, I can provide you with breads and sauces via overnight delivery. Go to my website at www.margauxsky.com and place your order. Breads, sauces, mixes, and other items will be delivered in time for your social affair.

INDEX